Wouldn't Mind Dying,
If Dying Was All

Wouldn't Mind Dying, If Dying Was All

Apostle Annie Davis/Duncan

DORRANCE
PUBLISHING CO
EST. 1920
PITTSBURGH, PENNSYLVANIA 15238

Dorrance Publishing Co
585 Alpha Drive
Pittsburgh, PA 15238
Visit our website at *www.dorrancebookstore.com*

ISBN: 978-1-6453-0173-3
eISBN: 978-1-6461-0535-9

I WOULD LIKE TO DEDICATE THIS BOOK
TO MY WONDERFUL MOTHER,

Dr. Luzine Stitts / Davis

She has been a great example and inspiration in my life.
She gave her life to Christ Jesus for her children and others.
She was a blessed woman of God.

ALSO, TO MY SOULMATE

Mr. Carl L. Duncan Jr.

He has always inspired me to do whatever
that the Lord has told me to do.
He has been by my side now for over 25 years strong.

THE TWO PEOPLE
THAT GOD HAS GIVEN TO ME
IN THIS LIFE
TO GROW GREAT IN THE LORD.

JESUS CHRIST THE SAME YESTERDAY,
AND TODAY, AND FOREVER...

Contents

Introduction

POEMS, DRAWINGS, SCRIPTURES, TESTAMONIES,
AND MIRACLES; SOME BIBLE STORIES BY
APOSTLE ANNIE R. DAVIS/DUNCAN...

I, Apostle Annie R. Davis/Duncan, decided to allow others to experience what goes on in my head, my thoughts, and feelings about living for Jesus. He has chosen and taught me the way that we should live while we are still in the flesh. We as people don't believe in anything unless we see it for ourselves. When we were born into this world, we had to learn how to do things in this life. It is the same way with Jesus Christ, our Lord and Savior. We have to learn how to live Holy and in the right standards with God. He has always been in my life and He has always made a way for me. But I haven't always been with the Lord Jesus. I had some good times and bad times, but I am so glad that I didn't wait too late to receive Jesus as the head of my life. The world is beautiful and heavenly made. We are made in the image of God Himself and He has created a whole world full of His image. With that being said, I believe that the world has a lot of love and compassionate human beings that still exists. People need to know that God is the head of all of our lives if we would allow Him to come inside of our bodies and lead direct our paths. I am not trying to change who you are serving or believe in. God has given us His Words to convert, convict, and change our lives. So, this is your decision and choice to choose Jesus as your Lord and Savior. When or if you read the Bible, which was inspired by God, then you will understand and grasp the concepts of life. Now I know without a shadow of a doubt that God is real and alive today, in our souls. He wants our minds and hearts to be pure with Him and ourselves. This is not a hard journey but a long one, and you can make it to the end with the help of Jesus Christ as your leader and guide.

This book is for all who believe and know that there is a God and His Son Jesus Christ, who loves, cares, and created all human beings and everything that exists. Just a few chapters to educate the ones who wants to learn and know about our Savior Jesus Christ our Lord. Take a small amount of time out of your life and read and study the words of God. It changed and rearranged my life, so I can live right here on earth in heaven. It wasn't anything that I had done or are doing to be blessed beyond blessed. He said in His Words "that there is no respect of person with Him Jesus." We all are treated equally in this world with God. There wasn't anything that I had done special or right, for Him to choose me to serve Him. It is a privilege and an honor to be chosen by God. In John the 6 chapter and 44 verse, it says, "No man can come to me, except the Father which hath sent Me draw him; and I will raise him up at the last day." Now this was Jesus speaking to us to let us know that we are chosen by God. We cannot come unto Him unless He chooses us. I learned from studying the different written words about God that we can live again with Him in His Kingdom. So, enjoy the book and know that there is a way that is better than the one that we living right now without Jesus. God giveth us the true bread from Heaven. For the bread of God is He which cometh down from heaven and giveth life unto the world.

Dr. Luzine Davis was a perfect example of how we as human beings are supposed to live until the judgment day comes. And the reason I chose her is because she allowed Jesus to change and rearrange her life. She also received the gift of the Holy ghost to keep her from sinning until her day was done and she slept away into His rest. But Jesus was our first example of how to live here on this earth. He taught us how to treat one another and how to react to struggles and trails of this world. I trust and believe that this little book will help someone out who is trying to get every blessing that the Lord has in store for them. Somebody truly wants to be saved, sanctified, and Holy ghost filled to live again with Christ Jesus. So, sit back and enjoy, learn and obey God's Word. God is who He says He is. He is our lives, we do not live until we allow Jesus to take control of our lives, show us how to live and love while we are in the flesh. This little book of notes will tell you what God said and how He wants us to live on this side. Heaven is my goal each and every day. Trust, believe, and know that you can be saved, perfect, and Holy ghost filled in the name of Jesus. Amen.

REVELATIONS OF THE KING JAMES BIBLE

SERMONS FROM THE DESKS OF DR. LUZINE DAVIS AND APOSTLE ANNIE DUNCAN -MIRACLES 2- DR. LUZINE DAVIS MIRACLE

I, Luzine, had a surgery in the 1900 of the year and had one of my ovaries removed. I was told by the doctors that I cannot give birth to anymore children, and I was still sexually active in my thirties. I truly believed that I could not get pregnant, so I didn't take anything to prevent any pregnancies. But God had a different plan and gave me a son at the age of 37. I cried for months because I was not married and I just knew that I was done with having children. This is the second miracle that was done on me by God. He has done so many miracles in my life that I am only going to share two of them. See, there is nothing impossible for God.

The very first one was when I was physically abused by my husband. We were not getting alone and I decided to leave and live with my mother and my three little girls. At that time, we had been married for over seven years, we were living with his mother and brother. My husband was not a good man for me and our children. So, I wanted out of the marriage so bad that I was willing to move in with my mother, although she lived in a two-bedroom duplex in Orange Mound area of Memphis.

One evening while we were sitting in the kitchen, trying to figure out what dinner was going to be. We begin to talk about our relationship and how we are not getting along with each other. So, I had made it up in my mind that we were going to leave each other, and he didn't agree with me for us to break up, so we begin to argue and fight until it got so heated up that we began to hit each other. Then I fell on the shift roll, which is a long wood box that holds all comforters and blankets, linens, etc. My head was laying on the rim of the shift roll and he stepped in my neck with all of his might and strength and broke my neck. My spinal cord almost split in half, but God had a plan for my life. My little girls screamed and cried out to his mother for help, but instead of helping me, she was complaining about us arguing and fighting. I finally was taken to the hospital John Gaston, the doctors didn't do very much because in that time, we didn't have any insurance for health coverage. I was looked at and they sent me home with the diagnose of being crazy and will not be able to walk or identify anyone anymore. They told my mother there wasn't anything that they could do for me. She was told to take me to the mental hospital and I wasn't going to be the same anymore. I couldn't talk, heard of a prayer service that was going on that week. So I wrote a note to my mother and told her to take me to the prayer service hosted by this lady named Sarah Steele, who was a very anointed woman of God. My mother took me to the service the next day and I already had faith that God will and can heal me. The moment that I got in the prayer line, my body and my neck started to tingle and feel hot. So, when it was time for her to lay her hands on me, the Lord God straightened out my neck and set my head back straight on my shoulders. I removed the neck brace and started praising Jesus, I started to shout and cry out thank you, Jesus. I recognized my children and knew who everybody was. I have been running for Jesus ever since. I know that God is real and true, so I gave him my life until He called me home on May 12th, 2016. Yes, God saved, sanctified, and Holy ghost filled me and I lived a blessed life. I received the Holy ghost at the late age of 53, felt like a fire ball hit me in the top of my head and I fell down on my knees. My whole body was hot on fire and I knew then that Jesus was giving me the gift of the Holy ghost to be kept until He called me in. (Deceased May 12th, 2016)

MIRACLES: APOSTLE ANNIE DUNCAN

I was born with a heart murmur the size of a quarter. I was told that if the murmur didn't close that I would have to have an open-heart surgery when I was 16-years-old. My lower part of my body swelled so big that I could not walk. I was taken to the same hospital that my mother was taken to when she had a trauma incident, John Gaston. We still didn't have great insurance but welfare medical insurance. They wanted to have surgery on me and cut open my chest to see what was going on. At first, the doctors said that I was bitten by a spider, they didn't have a clue why my body had swollen so big. But I had remembered that Pastor S. Steele prayed on my mother and she was healed, so I wanted her to pray on me, too. And she did and I was healed, my legs started to go down immediately after she anointed and prayed. But the faith that me and my mother had was outstanding and real. Cause God healed both of us. I also have had five surgeries on my stomach and God kept me and He healed me… I also was a victim of spousal abuse and the Lord got me out of the relationship without any harm done to me. There is no one in this world like the lonely Jesus, no, not one, I can't find one because I have been searching for a long time in my life to find love, joy, peace, and happiness. The only place and person that I found all of this is in Christ Jesus. I was on drugs, drinking, smoking, and fornications through-out my childhood and adolescence of life. But when I heard about Jesus, I knew that there was a better way in this life beside Hell on earth while the blood is running warm in my veins. I am very thankful for God's Son Jesus. I also had five surgeries on my stomach and God worked out a miracle, so I am still here at the age of 57 by giving my life to Christ Jesus. The most important thing about the miracles is that when God delivered you and restored your life is so awesome of a new life with Jesus. I need to let you know that not only did God heal me physically but mentally as well. It all started when I was a very young girl. I had been molested. Not to hurt or incriminate anyone with my story of life… God took my situation and turned all the pain and hate that I was feeling toward man and others. I had a hard and hurtful life as a child and Jesus was the only way that I was taught to heal and be whole as a human being again. I was taught at an early age about Jesus Christ and His Father God. So, I took and believe in everything that was taught to me about this Savior. Because of the abuse that was done to my mother and her children by our father and the child molestation that I received at an early age caused me to not trust in Jesus but to turn to drugs and alcohol. I was a drug addict for over ten years of my life. I got sick and tired of being used and misused by anyone I came in contact with. So, I decided to give Jesus another try. I gave all that had been done to me or against me to Jesus and I trusted that He will make it alright. I did not seek any counseling from anyone, nor did I go to a rehab to stop doing drugs. I went to Jesus and cried out with all my heart and soul and told God every wrong and everything that had happened to me in a loud secret prayer. Jesus heard my cry and He pity every groan, He immediately came and saw about me. He changed my way of thinking and my feelings about not wanting to live anymore. I owe all of my life and endeavors to Jesus. If it wasn't for the Lord, where or what would my life be. I could have been dead sleeping in my grave, but God had a plan for my life for His kingdom. He saved me from a burning hell and also from a life of misery and pain, suffering, and not wanting to be a part of the human race. I owe all of my strength and life to God. I now realize that I had to go through all of the trials and tribulations of life in order to be the person that God intended me to be. I thank Jesus everyday for what He has done for me. He washed and cleansed my sinful soul and made me a new creature in Christ Jesus. I am very grateful that He looked way down and picked me up and changed my heart from a black heart to a pure and clean loving heart. He also has given me the gift of the Holy ghost, so I can be kept on this earth until He returns for judgment. I have been given another chance of life and have experienced a full life with Christ. I had at least 32 jobs and owned two business and started a Ministry that lasted for over 16 years. I have been ordained and has ordained 16 people into the Ministry. Now I have been elevated to an Apostle level in Christ Jesus. So, yes, I am blessed and highly favored by Jesus Himself.

The material compiled in this mini booklet is to be a means by which to project a vision in the hearts and minds of teachers and learners of the Gospel of Jesus Christ (Habakkuk 2:2 says write the vision and make it plain upon tables, that he may run that readeth it). Our vision is to be excellent and to strive for excellence in the things pertaining to God and Kingdom business.

Topics of Dr. Davis Sermons:

- You Will Need a Spiritual Connection - (Before You Can Be Spiritual Reborn)

- 2 Seek Him Jesus to Receive a Spiritual Rebirth

- What Does Being Saved Means

- Live Holy Now and Forever

- God Servant's Can Not Sugar Coat His Gospel

- Jesus Was Sanctified Before He Did His Father Will

- There is Only One God

- Jesus is the Holy Word

- Who Are You Following?

- The Comforter

- Are You Seeking Jesus to Save You Holy?

These are sermons interpertation from the Holy Words by Dr. Luzine Davis and Apostle Annie Duncan.

Wouldn't Mind Dying, If Dying Was All

CHAPTER 1

Spiritual Connection

Spiritual Connection Before Spiritual Rebirth: In order to be spiritually reborn, you will need a savior, not a system to be saved. With a Spiritual Connection, you will serve others like Jesus did when He walked the earth. Most people often hope that others will meet their needs, we that are children of God should meet other needs in love, patience. When you don't have a spiritual connection with Christ, you are committed to your own ideas, not God's Holy Words. Some people are committed to their money and will trust in God as long as the money is convenient for them. These will refuse to give up their personal freedom, wealth, and statue. There is no way that these people will think to get a spiritual connection God. This is a great price to pay to give up the worldly values. Jesus told us to give up the material securities and follow Him (Luke 9:23, Matthew 16: 24, Mark 8:34, Luke 14:27).

This means that we have to deny ourselves by obeying Jesus. The things that we want to do is not the plan that God has for us. So, our plans for life in the world without Christ in it does not work or matter to Christ. We must pray daily, and throughout the day, read and study the Words of God. We must fellowship with our fellowman, fast, also be taught by a chosen person by God. Every preacher does not teach the true words of God. But He said try the spirit by the spirit to make sure that it is of

God. It's the same way as you are creating a relationship with another human being. Getting to know each other daily by spending time with that person. We have to make God our everyday priority to learn of Him Jesus. God should be our first daily agenda for life.

When it comes to serving God, you don't need a resume, you need a redeemer. I have learned that in this walk with Jesus, you must give Him your total attention concerning your life. He will lead and guide you in the right direction. Where to go, when to go, how to live, and how to obtain eternal life with Him Jesus. He also teaches us what to say and when to say whatever we have to say concerning anything in our lives.

Jesus said that if ye love the things of the world and sins of pleasure to the flesh, then the love of God is not living inside of you. You are just giving Him Jesus' lip service and playing church with Jesus and yourself (1John 2:15-17). Jesus wants to live down on the inside of us, not on the outside, nor behind your back or under your feet. He judges the heart of men, that's how He knows whether or not we are for real with Him. God is a choice, not a force, we have the right to the tree of life. Meaning that we don't have to continue to live in sin when Jesus has already paid for our sins. That's why we must be reborn into the Holiness of God. He that does will of God and allow Him to change your hearts and mind to live for Him. Then you will receive the gift of the Holy ghost from Jesus to keep you until His return.

CHAPTER 2

Seek Him to Receive a Spiritual Rebirth

A Spiritual Rebirth is an enlightenment causing a person to lead a new life, conversion, rebirth, redemption, salvation, the act of delivering from evil.

In this chapter, you will learn that we will have to allow Jesus to give us a Spiritual Rebirth in order to make it into the Kingdom of Heaven for an eternal life with Christ. You might ask yourself what is a Spiritual Rebirth? Well, this is when you allow Jesus to remove and rearrange all things in your life that is not like Christ. Even if it's takes you away from your so-called friends and family member. Serving the Lord is personal for you. We don't have time to think about whether not we still have plenty of time. Time waits on no one on this earth. Now is the acceptable time to give your lives to God. Why? Because the blood is still running warm in our veins, and when it runs cold, it is too LATE to seek and serve Him Jesus.

There is no other way for you to receive Christ. for the natural man receiveth not the things of the spirit of God, they are foolishness unto

Him, neither can he know them because the are spiritually discerned. But he that is spiritual judgeth all things, yet he himself is judge of no man. For no one knows the mind of the Lord that he may instruct Him Jesus. We have the mind of Christ we that are saved, sanctified, and Holy ghost filled with the nine fruit of the spirit. The Holy ghost teaches us what to say and we also live holy without sin before a Holy God, you cannot talk holiness, you got to live in God's holiness and His righteousness. Jesus said I am come that ye might have life and that ye may have it more abundantly to the fullness of God. God gave us eternal life through His Son, the Savior Jesus Christ. So, we can live for eternality, this world is sinful and evil corruption and death is forever present. If you are not saved, it is because you don't have faith in Jesus to save you. You have not received a Holy life, not the fullness of a Holy life in Jesus. The life that God gave us is the Holiness of Him. The Spiritual Rebirth will give you the Holy ghost for eternal life in God and His Son Jesus the power of everlasting exist only through our Lord and Savior Jesus Christ. If you are not fully equipped with the Holy ghost and the nine fruit of the Spirit, you will not experience the over flow of God's Holiness. The love, joy, peace, long suffering, gentleness, goodness, meekness, faith, and temperance. This was the reason that God sent His Beloved Son Jesus into this sinful world. to show you and I what a Holy life is about. You can receive eternal life now, He has given us time to choose whom we are going to serve and worship while we have time to make up our mind on who we are going to obey God or Satan. I pray that Christ may live in you by faith, so you will be strengthened with His Holy ghost power to line in the inner man is your belly (John 5:24), says verily, verily, means surly, surly, I, Jesus, say unto you, he that heareth my word and believeth on him that sent me hath everlasting life and shall not come into condemnation but is passed from death unto life (29 verse). And shall come forth and they that have done good, unto the resurrection of life; and they that have done evil, unto the resurrection of damnation (John 10:27). My sheep hear my voice and I Jesus know them, and they followe me (28 verse). And I Jesus give unto them eternal life; and they shall never perish, neither shall any man pluck them out of my hands. Jesus said the God has given Him choosen ones who no man can touch because God is greater than all; and no man can pluck them out of God's hand.

Jesus and God are one, you cannot come to God without going through Jesus first. God has given Jesus power over all flesh, that He should give eternal life to as many as thou hast given Him. Jesus glorified God on earth and He finished the work which God hasd given Him to do, which was to show us how to live and to teach us how to treat our neighbors and how to be kepted until He returns. He gave up His life on the cross was the last assignment was bestowed upon Jesus (1John 5:11) is the record that God hath given to us eternal life and this life is in His Son. So, if you have the Son, you hath life, and if you don't have the Son of God, you do not have life.

We were born in sin and shaped in iniquities, meaning that the flesh we have is sinful and evil. We have God's breath in us, but it was born sinful, so we have to allow Jesus to come in and cleanse us from our sins and evil ways to receive a Spiritual Rebirth from within. We have to repent daily, which means confess our sins and hate the sins that we are in. Then we must fast and pray about the things that are in our lives that are not like Jesus. Turn away daily from the worldly sins and Jesus can come in and sup with us. He will attend to our calls of help us to stop and come out.

When we fast for our Spiritual Rebirth, we must have faith and trust in Jesus to remove and destroy all unrighteousness that are not like Christ Jesus. We fast without telling anybody what we are fasting for and we wait patiently on Him to deliver us out of our sins that is so easily to beset us.

There are 59 bible verses about Spiritual Rebirth. There is only one body and one Spirit just as you were called to the hope that belongs to your call, one Lord, one faith, one baptism. If any man is in Christ, then he becomes a new man and the old man has gone away. No more sinning and leaning to the lust of your flesh.

CHAPTER 3

What Does Being Saved Mean

LIVING FOR JESUS CHRIST FOR REAL...
DON'T PLAY WITH GOD, HE IS A BUSINESS GOD

In this chapter, you will know that we only live when we have been saved. This means eternal life for us to live in the Kingdom with God. When you are saved, you will have sufferings, trials, and tribulations. But you will not go through your sufferings alone because you have some help and a keeper to help ease and carry you through your struggles. The devil cannot come near your dwellings, he cannot do anything to or against you without God's permission. Sometimes God allows the devil to carry us through some sufferings because God is trying to strengthen us or anoints us to a higher level in Him. Being saved means no more walks along, no more going a day without recognizing Jesus. When you are saved, you always acknowledge and allow Jesus to lead and guide your life. You don't do anything without consulting Jesus first. You bless everything you touch or do, you always pray and meditate on His words and Him. You love everybody and always see some good in everyone. You never change from being saved, you will always stay the same. When someone stands in need,

Jesus shows you how to or when to help. He also provides the materials or money for the help. You serve others and not yourself only. You always forgive and forget what a person has done against or to you. You stay in prayer daily to know what it is that you are suppose to be doing in that day. You walk the walk and talk the talk, your conversations are always Holy and affective. Your talk is season and good, you help with an understanding that you are not expecting anything in return. You pray for those who despitefully misuse you. Many people believe that you can save yourself, sin keeps you bound to Satan. Sin will not allow you to make it into Heaven nor receive peace while you are still here on earth.

Wisdom, knowledge, and understanding warning against enticement. These are the proverbs of King Solomon of Israel David's son. He wrote to teach his people how to live, how to act in every circumstance. For he wanted them to be understanding, just and fair in everything they did. He wanted to warn the young men and women about some problems that they will face.

Verses 7-9 in the first chapter of Proverbs, saying that to become wise is the first step to trust and fear the Lord. Only fools refuse to be taught, listen to your fathers and mothers. What you have learn from them will stand, it will gain you many honors with the Lord.

Verse 10 tells us that young people of evil will tell you to come on and join us. Turn your backs on them, they will say, let's hide and rob and kill. Then let's put our loot or money together and split it up equally. Don't do it for crime is their way of life and murder is their specialty. When a bird sees a trap being set, he stays away. We are more valuable than birds and have more human nature than they. But not these men and women they trap themselves, they lay like a booby trap for their own lives. Such is fate of all who live by violence and murder, they will die a violent death. Wisdom shouts in the streets for someone to hear her. She calls out to the crowds along the main streets, the judges in their courts, and to everyone in all the land.

Ye simple ones, how long will you go on being fools? How long will you scoff at wisdom and fight the facts? Come and listen to me, wisdom is pouring out the spirit of wisdom upon you. She says that I called you so often, but you still won't come. Some day you'll be in trouble and I'll laugh, mock me if you please and I will mock you. When the storm of terror surrounds you, when you are engulfed by anguish and distress. Then I will not answer your cry for help. It will be too late. These are the things that will happen to us when we don't adhere to our instructions from the Lord (Proverbs 1:1-33).

If you want to know what God wants us to do, ask Him and He will gladly tell you, for He is always ready to give a bountiful supply of wisdom to all who ask Him. He will not resent it, but when you ask Him, be sure that you are really expecting Him to tell you. For a doubtful mind will be unsettled as a wave of sea that is driven and tossed by the wind. Once you were under God's curse, doomed forever for your sins. You went along with the crowd and were just like all the others, full of sins, obeying Satan, the mighty prince of power of the air, who is at work right now in the hearts of those who are against the Lord. All of us used to be just as they are, our lives expressing the evil within us, doing every wicked thing that our passions or our evil thoughts might lead us into. We started out bad being born with evil natures and were under God's anger just like everyone else.

But God is so rich in mercy, He loved us so much that even though we were spiritually dead and doomed by our sins, He gave us back our lives again when He raised Christ from the dead-only by His undeserved favor have we ever been saved. And lifted us up from the grave into glory along with Christ, where sit with him in the heavenly realms. All because of what his Jesus did, and now God can always point to us as examples of how very, very rich his kindness is, as shown in all He has done for us through trusting Christ. And even trusting is not of yourselves; it, too, is a gift from God. Now when you trust someone to do something for you, you have faith in that person to do it. You believe that whatever you ask them, they will do it. So, God is the same way, you believe that whatever you need done in your life that He will do it. Having faith in God that He will and can save you from the sins of your life. He will and He can do it. But you have to give the sins to Him, repent for the sins, seek, pray, fast, study and serve Him. So, having faith that when I give my life to Christ, I will sit with Him in His Heavenly realms. One last thing we fail to do and realize it is part of the plan is to be helpers, one to another. There is no doubt about it because God said so and it is so. We must live, saved in order to make it into the kingdom of God.

CHAPTER 4

Living Holy Now and Forever

THIS IS THE ONLY WAY YOU ARE LIVING WHEN YOU LIVE HOLY WITH JESUS CHRIST FOR REAL..

Who are you obeying and who are you following?

When we go to church, what are we going for?

God wants us to live Holy and have more of an abundant life while we are in the flesh. He loves us so much that He came down from His Heavenly Home to show us how to live on this earth in the flesh. He is Real and a self-made Spirit. He made everything and He is a jealous God. He said that thy should have no other God before Him. Sometimes we don't know we are or have been putting before God. When we cherish our family, children, and material things before Him, we make Him very angry and upset at humankind.

In Jeremiah 3:14, He said, "Turn, o backsliding children, for I am married unto you: and I will take you one out of a city, and two of out a family, and I will bring you to Zion." He is saying that He will save one out of a city and two out of a family and give them life eternal. He also will give us preachers and teachers that will give us an understanding and knowledge of His words. He is God and He doesn't need our help, we need Him daily. The understanding of God is living without sins, but we have to receive the Holy ghost, the comforter to keep us Holy until He returns for His souls. He died in flesh, paid the ultimate price for our souls, and He wants it back Holy. Holy without no man shall see the Lord. Why, because He is a Holy God. Your talk, walk, living shall be Holy.

Try Jesus and see what He will and can do for you. Live everyday like it is your last day on this earth. No man or angel knows when, what, or where He is coming back for our souls. When a man dies, he can no longer serve or allow Jesus to abide. Our souls are immortal and lives forever. It has been given a choice to decide where we want our souls to live forever. Heaven or Hell is the question that we need to decide on. We have eternal life but who with or where. God is so true that He has a resting place for our souls until He returns with His Heavenly Hosts. We as preachers and teachers, also ministers, much feed the church of God, which He purchased with His own blood. Holy words are what God wants us to preach, not man ideals and tradition about His Holiness whether you hear and obey or not. We must express the disapproval of sins that lives in your life, we are to correct you in the Holy words and to encourage you with patience. You cannot get tired of preaching and living the truth of His Holiness.

Fear not them which kills the body but not able to kill the soul. People don't know or realize that the soul lives forever. We have been given a choice to choose where will our souls live when it is time for us to be judged. God is the rightful judge of our souls. He loves us so much that he has given us a choice to our souls. Now that's love because when we own something, we decide what to do with that thing that we own. But God gave us the right to the decision of something that He owns.

Now, I have been living without fear in this world because I know who owns this world. Jesus wants us to live in Heaven while we are still here on earth in our mortal bodies. But when it is time for our bodies to become immortality is when we will realize that there is a God.

Holy living is the only way to live on this earth, we are afraid of not being able to control what, when, where to go or do. We don't know our future, but God does. If we allow Him to come into our hearts and mind, then we will recognize that this way with Jesus is the best life ever. We learn how to worship Him in a Holy way, we learn how to live among the other flesh. He has taught us how to love one another with the true love that He has shown us. You might ask your selves how can I love when there is no love shown back? Well, it doesn't matter how others treat or love you because they cannot stand and be judge for you. It matters a whole lot how we treat or love one another. If you cannot love on this earth, then you can't love Jesus. Because Jesus is love and this is what makes the world go around. Because of the love that Jesus has for us.

Let me explain this situation for your understanding. God was angry about man's thoughts and his actions turned out. So, He had decided to give us one more chance to get it right. The bible said that it grieved God's spirit about humans beings (Genesis 6:6). The Lord regretted that He had made human beings on the earth, and His heart was deeply troubled. He looked on earth to find at least one human soul that was living righteousness before Him. He could not find one soul to redeem us back to His rest. That's when Jesus said prepare me a body and I will redeem man back to you. In order for this transaction to be Holy, He had to come down in a Holy and miracle way through a human body that has not been touched by man or mammon. So, He chose the little girl named Mary to be born through. If you cannot believe that God is real, I challenge you to try Him. Learn of Him, get a personal relationship with Him and you will find out and know without a doubt that there is a God. Many people believe that they can save themselves, sin keeps us bound to Satan. We get mad at God's words, but flesh cannot, God, it is an enemy to the Lord. Flesh has to die out of sin and be spiritual reborn with the Holy ghost spirit (John 8:34J). Jesus answered, "Verily, verily, means surly, surly I say unto you, whosoever committeth sin is the servant of sin." 36 verse of John 8 chapter also let us know that if the Son therefore shall make you free, ye shall be free indeed (Romans 5:21). That as sin hath reigned unto death, even so might grace reign through righteousness unto eternal life by Jesus Christ our Lord. So, we don't have to continue in sins, Jesus came so we can have rights to the tree of life through Him. Jesus spoke a lot about hell He is the only one who talked about it. There is a hell just like there is a heaven.

(Romans 6:1-2,7-8) What shall we say then? Shall we continue in sin that grace may abound? God forbid, how shall we that are dead to sin live any longer therein? For he that is dead is freed from sins, now if we be dead with Christ, we believe that we shall also live with Him Jesus. But there is another law in our bodies warring against the law of our minds and bringing us into captivity. If Christ be in you, the body is dead because of sin, but the spirit is life because of righteousness (Romans 8:13).

We have benefits that God promises for faithfulness, which is a Spiritual inheritance from God. Well, then knowing what lies ahead for us, you will not become bored with being saved nor will you become spiritually dull and indifference. But you will be anxious to follow the examples of those who received all that God has promised them because of their strong faith and patience with Jesus. For instance, there were God's promise to Abraham. God took an oath in His own name, since there was no one greater to swear by. That He would bless Abraham again and again and give him a son and make him the father of a great nation of people. Then Abraham waited patiently until finally God gave him a son who name was Isaac. When you take an oath, you are calling upon someone greater than yourself to force you to do what you have promised. God also bound Himself with an oath, so that those He promised to help would be perfectly sure and never need to wonder whether or not He might change His plans. God says He changes not. God has given us both His promises and His oaths, two things we can completely count on, for it is impossible for God to lie. Now all that run to Him to be saved can take new courage when you hear such assurance from God, you can know without a shadow of doubt that He will give you the salvation He has promised us. This certain hope of being saved is a strong and trustworthy anchor for our souls, connecting us with God Himself behind the sacred curtains of Heaven.

God has done so much for us on the cross. Jesus did what no one else can do. Jesus is the one and only one that can take away sins. Jesus did what the law couldn't do. He went down in hell and preached the gospel to the saints. His death made us free from sins.

The resurrection of Christ is the evidence of God's power. Jesus will thoroughly purge His flow, His blood made us free from sins and deaths. Being now justified by His blood, we shall be saved from God's wrath through Jesus. Anyone who gives up his home, brothers, sisters, father mother, wife, and children or property to follow Jesus shall receive a hundred times as much in return and shall have eternal life and blessings from God. Jesus' presence within us is God's guarantee that He really will give us all that He promised, and the Spirit seals upon us means that God has already purchased us and that he guarantees to bring us to Himself. This is just one more reason for us to praise our glorious God. Remembering that it is the Lord Jesus who is going to pay us, giving us His full portion of all He owns. We are working for Jesus to receive His reward of eternal life with Him.

CHAPTER 5

Have You Receved the Holy Ghost Since You Believed?

To the ministers, it is not confusion, the scriptures are clear and direct, also powerful. (John 7:38) says he that believeth on me, Jesus, as the scriptures hath said, out of his belly shall rivers of living waters. Talking about the Holy ghost, and at that day, you will know that I, Jesus, is in my Father and ye in me, and I in you. He that hath Jesus commandments and keepeth them continuely, it is that Loveth Jesus and he that loveth Jesus shall be loved of His Father and Jesus will love him and will manifest Himself to you.

Repent and be baptized, everyone of us in the name of Jesus Christ for the remission of our sins and ye shall receive the gift of the Holy ghost. We have a zeal of God but not according to the knowledge of God. We are the temple of God, the chapter 13 in the book of John is the teaching of the Comforter will come. Jesus said to us if ye love me, then keep my commandments.

John 13:26 teaches us that the Comforter, which is the Holy ghost, whom the Father will send in Jesus name, He shall teaches us all things and bring all things to our remembrance, whatsoever He Jesus had said unto us. We are the temple of God, and He will keep us with the same spirit and power.

When we start to go through the process of being saved, we must pray daily, read, and study His words to learn of Him and how to receive Him fully. Once He see us with a pure heart and mind, then He will come and attend to our needs and wants of Him. If you already been baptized and still sinning, then you need to be rebaptized into the Holiness of God. Meaning that you are seriously ready for Jesus to wash and cleanse your souls from sins. The next step is to fast for the Holy ghost to remove anything out of your lives that is not like Jesus. Study and read your words daily and worship with the Lord and fellowship with your members. Now you have to ask Jesus for patience and faith to believe that you will receive the Holy ghost to keep you Holy until He returns for your souls. The book of Psalms 63:1 says, "O God, thou art my God; early will I seek thee: my soul thirsteth for thee, my flesh longeth for thee in a dry and thirsty land, where no water is; blessed are thou which hungry and thirst after thee." This is David's cry for the Lord to fill him up with His Holy Spirit. So, you see that we have to want Jesus to live in us, so we can Holy and Righteousness before Him. We have to make Jesus our first priority when we rise up in the morning as soon as our sun comes up, which is our eyes open. Be hungry for His words as if you are hungry for food and water. Jesus calls us blessed if we search out and seek Him while we are able to acquire His righteousness. When you seek the Lord, you understand all things. Many seeks the ruler's favor, but every man judgment cometh from the Lord.

Then shall ye call upon, and ye shall go and pray unto me, and I will hearken unto you. He that speaketh of himself, speaketh of his own glory. The Holy ghost is an indwelling spirit, the nine fruit of the spirit means that you are living in the righteousness of God. Nevertheless the creation of God stands sure, having this seal means that God knows who are His. Let everyone that name the name of Christ come out from sin. If you don't want Christ in your life, then why do you want to spend eternity with Him? Because when you receive the Holy ghost, He will testify of Jesus. He will guide you into all truth, He will not speak of Himself, He will show you of things to come (John 16: 13-15).

Matthews 15 chapter talks about how we come to Jesus with lip service and not from the heart. We draw nigh unto Jesus and honorth Him with our lips, asking for Him to save us and not really wanting the process that is required to be saved. Jesus wants us to be sanctified because His words are true. (John 3:3) says surly, surly I, Jesus, say unto thee except a man be born again he cannot see the kingdom of God. Cause whosoever is born of God doeth not commit sin, for his seed remaineth in him and he cannot sin. You must receive the Holy ghost in order to make it into Heaven, Holy without no man shall see the Lord (Hebrews 12:14).

So, you see that we must get saved, complete and living a perfect will in the Lord. The first step is to repent and be baptized in order to move forward in God. Jesus has some work to do on us, like giving us a Spiritual rebirth in Him. Changing our way of thinking and living for Christ. There is no other way to get into the Kingdom of Heaven. One God, one faith, and one baptism, Father, Son, Holy ghost, which is the most important process in getting saved. The Holy ghost is a He and He is a keeper of our souls, to be kept until Jesus' return. A comforter in the time of sorrow and a teacher of the words of God.

CHAPTER 6

Christ the Way of Life

The first answer that I can give is that our souls belongs to God Himself. We were born with His Holy Spirit, but the spirit needs to be reborn into the Holiness of God. God is powerful and two positive energies cannot exist in the same vale at the same time. Unless one of the energies allows the other to exist. So, in order for that to happen, we have to deny self and allow Jesus to come into our hearts and bodies. God is so REAL that He thought of everything we need to survive in this world. We were born in sin and shape in inequity. This means that we are sinners first before we are Saints and we have evil tendencies. He created good and evil from the beginning of the world. This is God's world and all the people that dwell there in. So, we must realize that Jesus is in control of it all. If you decide not invite or allow Jesus into your life, then keep on doing whatever it is that you are doing in this world. Because Jesus is not mad at your choice or nether does He do any drive bys to make us accept Him into our lives. He just knows what He has created and what it will take for His creations to live truly on this earth with Him. Without Jesus in our lives, people don't know that our souls are eternal, means that the body gets old and sometimes dies out like withered grass that has died and gone away. But our souls are forever and needs a place to rest. And we want our souls to rest in peace until the day of judgment comes. But in order for us to receive that rest in Jesus, we must sell out and give our lives to Him.

When we recognize that our lives are nothing without Jesus, He is our everything. He teaches us to love for real on each other, shows us that there is nothing impossible without God. Our minds and thoughts are not like God, it doesn't even come close to His. It took me a long time in my life to know that I needed the Lord. Sometimes we make the wrong and tough decisions that cause us to lose out on our own lives. God has given us a choice because that's the only way that we can show our love for Him and each other's. We don't understand why He did it, but I just know that I am glad that He did. We are the puppets and He is the puppeteer, the owner, and the only one who showed us love by dying on the cross for all of our sins. This redeemed us back to God's love. So, you see it is very important that we make a choice about whom we are going to serve. I choose Jesus after He chose me, I didn't know that He had a plan for my life. I was born to serve Him, but in order for His plan to execute, I had to go through all the heartache and pain, the struggles and temptations that I endured with Jesus on my side. I didn't know that He had chosen me to be His servants, especially after all the sins that I had done while I was yet in my youth. Let me testify about what I have been through while I was just a little girl living in sin. I used to do drugs, I smoked cocaine, crack, weed, took pills, and drank alcohol and beer. Also smoked cigarettes and heroin. I also sold my body for drugs, I lied, cheated, and stole things that did not belongs to me to support my habits. Because that's what all those things were, some habits, but those habits caused my body not to function the way that it was designed to do. And the habits caused me to get far from Jesus and live to the lusts of my flesh. Then I heard a loud voice in my head that told me to live for Him from that point on in my life. Now don't get me wrong, but I didn't obey Jesus as soon as I heard Him spoke to me. It took me another 10 to 15 years to give Jesus my total life. Now I don't know that was His plan, but I learned that it is our decision whether or not we answer when He calls our name. If I had answered His call when I was in my 20's, then I believe that I could have brought more people to the thrown of grace, so I learned that it is our faults when we stand in the way of sinners or sit in the seats of scornful. We must pray daily and meditate day and night on His Word and on Him.

I learned how to live Holy and I also learned how to fast for the things that were in my life that was not like Christ Jesus.

There is a whole lot of information in the bible that will lead and guide us to the right choice, which is Jesus. If you love to read about love stories, drama, happiness, peace, joy, and how to live in the right standards of Jesus, it's in the Words of God. Some people might question how do you know that God or Jesus is real? Well, my answer to that question is because when I started to seek, knock, and ask Him questions, He heard me and answered me. He changed my life. I did not go to no rehabilitation center or counsel with no preacher or bishop. I went to Jesus, just like I was with all of my sins and while I was still in my sins. I searched Jesus out every day for years until I started to see and feel a change in my life that felt better than what I was doing. Every time I called His name, He came and talked to me and held me in His arms. He did miracles in my life for as me being a sick girl from birth. I had it hard and didn't know that all I had to do was try Jesus for real. I'm not talking about just going to church or bible study and go back home the same way that I left to go to the meetings about Christ.

He, Jesus, gives us gifts and talents, also life. Without Jesus we are walking around this earth dead, we just had not been buried yet cause the blood is still running warm in our veins. This is when He can use us while the blood is still warm in our veins. Cause once the blood goes coldm we cannot work or seek for salvation in Jesus. In the book of John, 14th chapter tells us that we should not trouble about the things of this world that we cannot control. It says let not your hearts be trouble and the reason why Jesus said that we should not trouble ourselves is because He has already prepared a resting place for our souls if we believe in Him, Jesus. And though word believe is not just saying it in your minds or just believing and not trusting in Jesus to save you fully to receive eternal life. When Jesus died on the cross for our sins, that's not the only thing that needs to happen for eternal life with Christ. We have to seek out and learn the ways of life that Jesus expects us to live. We to know without a shadow of a doubt that He can and will save us Holy. Holy without no man shall see the Lord, and the word shall is a continue word that means you will not see God without being Holy. He wants us to come as we are, which means whatever sin that we are doing or in Jesus wants us to bring them to Him, so He can wash them clean and renew a right spirit in us and cleanse our hearts for the work of the kingdom. He also said in my father's house are many mansions. He is not talking about an actual house or rooms. He is talking about there is so much space in the Lord, and if you give Him your souls, then there is a place for your souls to rest until the day He returns. In order to have a belief in Jesus, you have to allow Him to come into your lives and hearts and change it to an Holy vessel. Flesh and blood is not what He requires. He wants our souls because He paid the utter most price for the souls. Jesus did what no other human could do. In the old days before Jesus came on the scene, there was no human living what was expected for the humans to live. Every time they offer up a sacrifice and still went back to sinning. The Lord have never seen the righteous for saken or His seeds beg for bread. So, knowing this that Jesus is our Shepard and a Shepard takes care of his sheep. We have to make sure that we are His sheep and not goats. Because goats don't make it into heaven. A goat is a synonym of the ones who do not wants to be saved. The ones who want to live life as they choose, going about establishing their own righteousness and not the righteousness of God. He said that my people perish from lack of knowledge. We have to acknowledge Jesus in all of our ways everything that we do is possible because of Jesus. We have to learn how to live on this earth while we are in the flesh. We have to repent and turn from the things that are not like Christ. Seek Him daily to save us from a burning hell. Learn how to love one another with God's love because our love will tell us the moment that we are misused or abused. The love of God never fails or change, so we needs that same love to be able to continue in Jesus. It is not a hard decision to make about who we are going to serve. God gave us this choice because He loves us, despite of all the sins that we have commented. The reason why like I have mentioned in other chapters is that we were born with His spirit but that spirit that we were born with is sinful. Sin is not going to make it into the kingdom of God, God doesn't deal with or allow any sins into his kingdom. Man turned away from God over 2,000 years ago and is still turning away.

When we realize that it is God that has us here, it is God that allows us to continue to live in our sins. God has all power in His hands, man or woman cannot do or live without God's say so. People give the devil a lot of credit for God's actions or doings. God is the head man in charge of us and all the planets that He created. When we realize that the power is an unsearchable power and that God is a self-made Holy Spirit and He controls all that is good or evil. We cannot breathe without God's say so or even move without Him. God has a plan for His creations and if we don't walk in the plan of the Lord, then we are going to be lost in this world of sin.

I made a vow and took an oath that I will tell a dying world that Jesus is and lives in our souls. People don't want to hear or be told the truth about how to live or how to receive an Spiritual Rebirth in order to make into Heaven to get eternal life. Most of them that preaches or teaches the words of the Lord have not received the Holy ghost. And that's why this world is in so much evil and tumors, trails and tribulations, also suffering alone without Jesus. When you suffer with Jesus, you will not go through a hard ship suffering. Neither will you be saddened or lost with Jesus. He is the only way for us to live and have a prospers and abundance life on this earth. You cannot succeed in this world and have the right standards without Jesus in your lives. I don't write with enticing words or big unexplainable words to confuse you. I write and teach, so a fool will not err, or a two-year-old child can understand the way to the Lord.

Don't you yet understand, don't you know by now that the everlasting God the Creator never grows weary or faint. No one can fathom the depths of His understanding. He gives power to the tired and worn out, and he gives strength to the weak. Even the youths shall be exhausted, and the young men will all give up. But those that wait upon the Lord, He shall renew their strength. They shall mount up with wings like eagles; they shall run and not be weary, they shall walk and not faint. Being still waiting on something. Not moving to your ideals but taking actions to the will of God. Having faith substance of things, hope for evidence of things not seen. After you waited and knowing having faith, now God can move on your behalf. Many will see and know that it was God's glory and wonderful works, and they will be fearful about Him. Now they will put their trust in God. If He did it for me, He will do it for you because there's no respect of person in God's eyes. Everybody has the right to the tree of life. Rest in the Lord and wait patiently for him to act. Don't be envious of men who prosper evil. Don't repay evil for evil, wait on the Lord to handle the matter. Pray for them who despitefully misuse you and say all manner of evil against you. Isaiah

40:21-22 asks are ye so ignorant, are you so deaf to the words of God? The words He gave before the world began. Have you never heard nor understood?

It is God who sitteth above the circle of the earth. He is the one who is in control and stretches out the Heavens like a curtain and make His tent from them.

CHAPTER 7

Sheeps and Goats

My vision is to be excellent and to strive for excellence in the things pertaining to God and God's kingdom and business. Sometime we need to stop and ask ourselves the questions: whose kingdom are we building? Who are we going to serve?

The bible tells us without a vision the people perish. We must examine ourselves often, to judge our own characters for we are the Church of God. We are the members of Jesus Christ's body. If we are not allowing God to live in our bodies, then we belong and are building the devil's kingdom. And we all have choices, so who's kingdom are you building? The sheep are to the right side of Jesus and the goats are to the left side. The word also tells us that if you are just, then stay that way, just. And if you are unjust, then stay unjust because you cannot be both a sheep and a goat. You cannot serve two masters, you hate one and love the other. You can't love on two, it will not work. And you are still saying yes, I can swing with the devil on the weekend and hangout with Jesus on Sunday or the day you choose to worship Christ. But the problems with that is each master has rules and order. Swinging with the goats and devil requires all of the sins that you can fit into your life. Not having an understanding of the things of the world and your fellowman. Not forgiving without forgetting, having things on the earth that will not allow you to have or receive eternal life with Christ.

Now Jesus requires us to pray, read, study, and learn of Him and His ways of living in the flesh. To mediate on Him and His words daily, He gives us a guide for everyday living with Christ. To love one another, to forgive and forget what have been done to you from others. So, you can't have two masters, God gives us a choice: love me, Jesus, or reject me, Jesus. But you might say, well, I want to love Jesus, but I'm not ready yet. I still have more life to live. He tells us in His words that the day that we hear His voice harden not our hearts. This means that when you have got sick and tired of being sick and tired. God answers your prayers, but you've got to listen to Him when He speaks to you. Through His words or through the preachers and teachers of His words. He is saying so many times in different ways to come on in and let me save you Holy to live and have eternal life with Him, Jesus. So, don't act like you don't know that God is speaking to you. When you do this, you are hardening your hearts to Him. Set your eyes on heavenly things of this world. The sins of this world are temporary, not forever, and will lead you into damnation and destructions of your souls.

God promised His sheep that if we live for Him that we would have joy, peace, long suffering with Him and heaven on this side while the blood is still running warm in our veins. Because one day on our day of dying, the blood will not run warm but cold, and it will be too late to become a sheep of the Lord's. He will give you whatever your hearts desires when you give Him your lives. God cannot lie, nor is He a man that He must repent. I advised you to obey the Holy ghost's instructions and you will have eternal life with Jesus. Galatians 5:16.

The earth belongs to God, everything in all the world is His. He is the one who pushed the oceans back to let the dry lands appear. Who may climb the mountain and enter where He lives? Who may stand before the Lord? Only those with pure hands and hearts who do not practice dishonesty and lying. They will receive God's own goodness as their blessings from Him, planted in their lives by God Himself, their Savior. These are the ones who are allowed to stand before the Lord and worship the God of Jacob.

Jeremiah 8:15, 20 says we expected peace, but no peace came; we looked for health, but there was only terror. The harvest is finished, the summer is over, and we are not saved. The getting ready, the planting, digging, and the plucking up is through. No more time to plant and pluck up. No more time to work or not work, the time has come the heat is gone, the resting is over. The laying around and vacationing is over. Did you plant where you were supposed to plant? Did you water where water was needed? Did you put off or pluck up when it was time to? No more working, no more vacationing, no more clocking in or clocking out. The time has come, are you ready? Only the ones who has worked for Jesus, obeyed, been honest about themselves, love where there were hate will get in.

MATTHEWS 25:30-4

Throw the useless servants out into outer darkness; there shall be weeping and gnashing of teeth. The Messiah (the son of man). But when He shall come in, all of His Glory and all the nations shall be gathered before Him. And He will separate the people as a shepherd separates the sheep from the goats. A sheep is a humble creature. A goat is a wild and roughly creature. Both animals live on the same farm, but when the day comes to take them to sell or judge, they have to be separated. Who are the sheep and goats? We are all God's people, but the sheep will inherit the kingdom of God. They are in the will of God. The sheep took care of and looked out for God through His people. God spiritually don't need anything but fleshly He does (earthly). Your fellowman, whatever you do to one another, you do it to God. To become a sheep for the Lord, you must give Him your lives, allow Him to come into your hearts and mind, souls. Love one another, take care of one another. When someone is naked and hungry or homeless, you must do all that you can to help. When someone is sick and can't do for themselves, you must help whether it is to give them just a drink of water and pray for them to be healed.

How to be a goat is simple, just don't obey God's words and will. Keep on sinning and doing what your evil nature is telling you to do. When you are blessed with more than enough, you keep it all to yourself. The goat goes into everlasting punishment. The sheep are righteousness into everlasting life that provides eternal life with Christ Jesus.

CHAPTER 8

Trails and Temptations

JAMES 1: 1-17

A temptation. Succeed in this life by trusting and believing in God Almighty. Let me name a few, Joseph was a great example of temptation, and Job was an excellent of trails.

This epistle is from James, a servant of God and of the Lord Jesus Christ. James wrote this epistle to the Jewish Christians scattered everywhere. And to us as well because we were grafted into the inheriting of God. Is your life full of difficulties and temptations? Then be happy or glad that it is. Then you say to yourself, why? Why should I be happy when I am going through my trails and temptations? Knowing this, if you don't know anything else. Know that when the way is rough, your patience has a chance to grow. Because without trails and temptation, your patience cannot grow. And you need for your patience to grow. So, let it grow and don't squirm or work out your own problems. When your patience is finally in full bloom, then and only then you will be ready for anything, you will be strong in character. Full and complete, when you have patience, you can wait and trust in God. If you want to know what God wants you to do, just ask God! And He will gladly tell you. For God is always ready to give a bountiful supply of wisdom to all who ask Him, not leaning on your own understanding. But trusting in God, liberally and upbraiding, meaning that He has a generous spirit in helping the needy, upbraided means He will criticize and find fault and help you to straighten out your problems. And He will not resent showing and helping you.

But when you ask, make sure that you are ready to receive what He has to give or tell you. You must believe and have faith in whatever He has for you. A doubtful mind is unsettled as a wave of the sea that is driven and tossed by the wind. Not knowing where you are going or what you are doing. Every decision that you make will be wrong and uncertain. You go this way and that trying to make the right decisions. If you don't believe in what you are asking, then God will not show or handle the situations. You want get an answer from God. Why, because you don't believe that He can fix it. If you don't amount much or have nothing or doing alright. You should be glad and shouting to the world because you are great in the Lord's sight.

You see that word blessed is the man, the word man that learn and trust in God for all things. Even when it comes to trails and temptations, the man just holds on to his faith and doesn't give in to the wrong doings when he is tempted. For afterwards he will get the crown of life. The success of living on earth, as God has promised those who love Him. And when you love Jesus, you will believe in Him and obey His commandments. When God says hold on and don't give up or out or in to your tests or temptations. He will bring you out. Look at verse 13, it said when you want to do wrong, it is never God who is tempting you, for God never does wrong or He never tempts anyone to do wrong or right. So, Jesus doesn't tempt you to lust, you decide this on your own. Temptation is the pull of man's own evil thoughts and wishes. God made the body and designed it. But we are the ones who initiates the pleasures of our flesh. God didn't give us organs and said don't use them. He gave us instructions on how to use them to His glory, not ours. He even told us with whom we can use them with and how.

See, evil thoughts lead to evil actions, and after that, evil action is a death penalty from God. Once you come up with the way that you think and feel how you should be satisfied, that is what you act on and defy God's order. Pleasing yourself the way that you want to be pleased. And not allowing God's way to work, not even trusting in the way that He designed sex to please, pleases you. God's way is not enough, we want it and it is not God's way. So, now you have to die in sin for being disobedient to God and hell burns forever.

Since you know this, don't be misled, don't do wrong on purpose. Knowing this, the trying of your faith worketh patience. When you have patience and wait on Jesus, you will succeed in life doing things and accepting temptations and not going through trails of life trusting in God causes you to burn in hell. All good and perfect gifts come down from God, the creator of all light, and He shines forever change or shadow. It was a glorious day for God when He gave them new lives and grafted us into His own free will. Through the truth of His word, and we became as it were, the first children in His new family as well. Listen to the life and story of the two men that obeyed God's order and went through their trails and temptations.

We think that we are the only ones who have hatred in our family or jealousy in our circles. We all have division in our lives, whether it be family or friends. But we must know how to get the divisions worked out. Joseph family brothers didn't like what God has made him to be. People always wants to change you to fit their needs. Like they made you, or breathe breath of life into you. You have to be as they want you to be. Not be what God has made you to be, and a lot of us had done or will do something to try to change others to their expectation of life. Not accepting people for who they are and loving and praying for them anyway. So, they try to fix you or disown you. Mislead you or do you wrong, but they don't know that they are blessing you, now you have to lean and depend on Jesus.

THE STORY OF JOSEPH'S TEMPTATION: (GENESIS 39)

I chose this story of Joseph because he was just a normal and natural man. We know the story of the temptation of Jesus by the devil. But I wanted you to know that there's no respect of person when it comes to God. We all were tempted some point or another in our lives.

When Joseph arrived in Egypt as a captive of the Ishamelite traders, he was bought by Potiphar, meaning that Potiphar owned Joseph, and Potiphar was a staff of Pharaoh, the king of Egypt. The chief executioner of Pharaoh, Pharaoh's bodyguard. God blessed Joseph while he was in the house of his master Potiphar. Everything that Joseph did prospered,

Potiphar noticed and showed that the Lord was with Joseph in a very special way. So, he put Joseph in charge of the administration of Potiphar household and all of his business affairs. Immediately, God begins to work for Potiphar because of Joseph trusting and loving God. All of Potiphar's house begins to run smooth. He didn't have a care or worry in this world because of Joseph being there and in charge.

But one day, Potiphar's wife began making eyes at Joseph and wanted him to come and sleep with her. But Joseph refused the offer, he told her that his master trusts me with everything in the entire household; he himself doesn't have more authority than I. He has held nothing back from me, except for you, his wife. How can I do such a wicked thing as this? It would be a great sin against God. See how Joseph was a faithful man and trusting in God. Why, he knows what God says about fornicating and sin. He didn't worry or thought about what Potiphar will say or how he will feel. His first thought was what will this do against God's law.

But every day after that, she kept on asking him to have sex with her, day after day. He continued to refuse and stayed out of the way of her as much as possible. One day they were in the house and no one was in the house but her and Joseph. She grabbed him by the sleeve, demanding that he sleep with her. He tore himself away, but as he did, his jacket slipped off and she was left holding it as he ran from the house. When she saw that she had his jacket, he was running to see what was happening. "My husband brings this Hebrew slave into our house and he just insulted us!" she said to the guards and her husband. Potiphar threw Joseph into prison, but God showed him favor while he was in prison. God put Joseph over the entire prison affairs, and God took care of Joseph while he was locked down in jail. God made the King come and ask Joseph for trails and will never have to worry about your life or what will you do nor the trails of this world will not cause you to lose faith in Jesus. Since the King Pharaoh was pleased in Joseph's services to him, he gave Joseph a ring for authority and dressed Joseph in beautiful clothing and gave him royal golden chain on his neck, then he put Joseph in charge of all of the land of Egypt.

Joseph resisted his temptation of fornication and came out a winner at the finishing line. God also did great things in his life concerning the way his brothers treated him.

THE TRAILS OF JOB: (JOB 1-3 CHAPTERS)

I chose Job because he was a man after God's own heart, he was just an upright man who feared the Lord and was perfect in the eyes of God.

He was one of God's own, he had to go through trials and tribulations to make his patience grow strong for God to know that he does love Him. So, God took him through the greatest trails of this world. He killed all of Job's children at one time together, and God took everything that Job had. Job was stricken with an illness, a sickness that none of us can stand or take. His flesh fell from his bones, he lost all of his cattle and servants. Job told God though you slay me, I am still going to wait on the Lord. Having faith and knowing without a shadow of doubt that God is going to come through for you no matter what happens to you. That moved the hands of God, and He blessed Job with more than he had at first. But his own wife wanted him to curse God and die, but he refused her and told her that she talked like a foolish woman, she said you have to go through till the end of the race. Through all of the obstacles and suffering that is required for us to go through. We must carry our cross, but we don't have to carry it alone. We need Jesus in our lives to bare our burdens. Just because you think you're big or better than God. Job thought that since he was after God's heart and perfect and upright man that he was excused from the trails, tests, and suffering of Christ. When Job tried to tell God all that he has done for Him, God asked him these questions: (Job 38:4-7) where were you when......? Who is man that I should be mindful of? Or how faithful that he has been. It is God's will to do whatever He wants to do and to whom He wants to do it to.

CHAPTER 9

The Right Kind of Faith

I must teach and preach the kind of faith that will lead people to have faith in the Lord Jesus Christ. You cannot place the faith of people in the wisdom of men but in the power of God's Spirit. (1 Corinthains 2:5) The wisdom of men cannot save man. Only the power of God can, it is of no value whatsoever for a man to just acknowledge that Jesus lived, that He was an historical person. Or that Jesus is the Savior, He is truly the Son of God. That other human knowledge and wisdom of men, also human arguments and appeals, may seem rational and logical, but they have no spiritual power. No person, speech, and no preaching can convert a human soul and impart eternal life to it. Only God can do such a thing, anything short of God's spirit places a person's faith in the knowledge and wisdom of men.

Hebrews 11:1 tells us that now faith is the substance of things hoped for, evidence of things not seen. This is saying the confident assurance that something we want is going to happen, it is certainty that what we hope for is waiting for us, even though we cannot see it up ahead.

You must make sure absolutely sure that your belief in Christ is the right kind of belief (John 3:16).

Romans 10:9-10: For if you tell others with your own mouth that Jesus Christ is your Lord and believe in your own heart that God has raised Him from the dead, you will be saved. For it is by believing in your hearts that a man becomes right with God, and with confirming his salvation. There are so many revelations in these two verses of whether or not you are saved. The word will be, and believing in your hearts are very powerful words. The words will be means that there is something that we have to do, and believing in your hearts means that we must be real and sure in what we believe. There is a process that we must go through in order for us to truly believe in Jesus. And that process is learning, studying, fasting, repenting, praying, seeking, asking, knocking, leaning, and trusting in what Jesus say He will and can do and also allowing the transformation and change. So, it is more than just a belief.

Hebrews 11:6 reads that you can never please God without faith without depending on Him Jesus. Anyone who wants to come to God must believe and know that there is a God and He rewards those who sincerely look for Him. God judges the hearts of men.

Saving faith is not this:

- Is not head knowledge, not just a mental conviction and intellectual assent expressing an approval or agreement.

- It is not just believing in history, that Jesus lived upon earth as the Savior.

- Believing the fact that Jesus Christ is the Savior

- Just believing the words and claims of Jesus in the same way that a person would believe the words of Obama.

Saving faith is:

- Believing in Jesus Christ who and what He is. That He is the redeemer of life with your whole hearts. Believe so much in such a degree that you will give your whole life body and soul to Him. Confess Jesus and turn your lives over completely and totally to live for Him, Jesus.

- Commitment is your total being and life to Jesus, it is the commitment of all you are and have to Christ. You will give everything to Jesus, even your affairs. You trust Him to take care of all of your past sins and your present welfare, your future destiny. Possessions and every part of you will be entrusted to Jesus.

- Daily necessities and acknowledging Him in all of the ways of life. You will follow Christ in every area in every detail of life, seeking His instructions and leaving your welfare up to Him.

Being obedient to faith, we have received grace and apostleship, for obedience to the faith among all nations for His name. Paul said that by him being a prisoner of the Lord, beseech you that ye walk worthy of the vocation where with ye are called. With all lowliness and meekness, with longsuffering, forbearing one another in love.

There is one body, one spirit, even as ye are called in, one hope of your calling. One Lord, one faith, one baptism. One God and Father of all, who is above all, and through all, and in you all. But let us, who are of the day be sober, putting on the breastplate of faith, and love and for a helmet the hope of salvation (1 Thessalonians 5:8).

It is not enough to just believe in Jesus and not use the saving and right kind of faith. A lot of us say and know that Jesus is the Son of God, that He died for our sins. This is not enough to make it into Heaven. We have to exercise our saving faith and allow Jesus to provide for us, to keep us and to show us the right kind of faith to have. Faith is what saves you, you have to walk, talk, and live by faith. Knowing without a shadow of doubt that God can and will remove all things that is not lined up to receive His salvation. That He will give you a spiritual rebirth and you can be born again.

Why do we make sure to the lust of the flesh that we have enough of everything that the body calls for, wants, and needs?

- Enough Food - to get full, sometimes too much gluttony

- Gas - to get where we are going, to make it there and back

- Soap - to wash the body, to make sure that it smells good

- Cigarettes - not to run out, but if we do, we go and buy more.

- Weed - to get high on, we buy enough to feel good

- Sex - to fulfill our sexual desires, we find the right mate to sleep with, so our desires and lusts are filled.

- Clothes - to wear so we will not be naked, different outfits and shoes.

- Money - to get the things that we want, to be able to go and do the things of this world for entertainment.

- Hair Supplies - to make sure that our hair is fixed the way we want.

- Enough Time - to kill, steal, to be idle, and do nothing

But we don't make sure that we get enough of saving faith the right kind of faith to get into Heaven where our Heavenly Father is or get salvation. We don't make sure the real us, which is our souls, gets all of the supplies that it needs to continue to live eternally with Christ. The corruptible flesh gets all of the attention from us to survive in this world. But the incorruptible soul gets NOTHING!

Jesus said why are ye so fearful of things when they arrive in your life? How is it that ye have no faith? To fulfill what the flesh calls for. The right faith for your souls you don't have.

Jesus, who being in the form of God, thought it not robbery to be equal with God. Though He was God, did not demand and took the rights as God. But made Himself of no reputation and took upon Him the form of a servant and was made in the likeness of men. He, becoming like men. In the likeness of men, being found in fashion as a man. He humbled Himself and became obedient unto death, even the death of the cross dies as a criminal's death on a cross. Wherefore God hath highly exalted Jesus and given Him a name, which is above every name. That at the name of Jesus, every knee shall bow, every tongue gonna confess that Jesus Christ is Lord, for God so loved the world that He gave His only begotten Son that whosoever believeth in Him should not perish but have everlasting life.

We have great faith in the things of this world, we eat, sit down, drink, walk, and talk. Put chemicals in our hair, make plans for what we are going to do the next day or year, not having the right kind of faith to get us saved. God can remove and change our lives to live Holy and acceptable unto Him. You can never please God without faith.

For it is by believing in his heart that a man becomes right with God, and with his mouth, he tells others of his faith confirming his salvation. Being obedient to faith the way the scriptures says that by whom we have received grace and apostleship for obedient to the faith among all nations for His name.

CHAPTER 10

Dead to Sins Alive in Christ

Well then, shall we keep on sinning, so that God can keep on showing us more and more kindness and forgiveness? Of course not, should we keep on sinning when we don't have to? Sin's power over us was broken when we were baptized to become a part of Jesus Christ; through His death, the power of sinful nature baptism when He died. And when God the Father, with glorious power, brought Him back to life again, you were given His wonderful new life to enjoy. For we have become a part of Him, and so you died with Him, so to speak, when He died. And now you share a new life and shall rise as he did.

ROMANS 6:1-23

The 6 verse says that your old evil desires were nailed to the cross with Him; that part of you that loves to sin was crushed and fatally wounded, so that sin loving body is no longer under sin's control, no longer needs to be a slave to sin. This is telling us that we were born in sin and shaped in evil and desires to sin. When Jesus died on the cross, He gave us the right to be reborn into His Holiness. He paid the price that His Father said that was required for us to have that right to the tree of life. We are loved by God and He had provided a way for us to get eternal life through His Son Jesus. Christ rose from the dead and will never die again, death no longer has any power over Him. Jesus died once for all to end sin's power, but now He lives forever in unbroken fellowship with God. Don't let sin continue to control your puny bodies any longer; do not give in to its sinful desires. Parts of your bodies wants to become tools of wickedness, to be used for sinning. But give yourselves completely to God. Every part of you for you are back from death and you want to be tools in the hands of God, to be used for His good purposes.

Sin need never again be your master, for now you are no longer tied to the law where sin enslaves you, but you are free under God's favor and mercy. Now you are free from your old master, sin, and you have become slaves to your new master, righteousness. The perfect will of God the Father, it is the only way that you can have a peace of mind knowing that you will make it into Heaven is a peace within itself.

Christ made us free, now make sure that you stay free by receiving the gift of the Holy ghost, which is given by Jesus. Try not to get tied up again in the chains of slavery of sin, but continue to seek and search out your soul's salvation. Listen to me, for this is serious, if you are counting on clearing your debt to God by keeping those laws from back, then you are lost from God's grace. But we by the help of the Holy ghost are counting on Christ deaths to clear away our sins and make us right with God. I advise you to obey the Holy ghost's instructions. He will tell you where to go and what to do, and then you won't always be doing the wrong things your evil nature wants to do. So, when the Holy ghost controls your life, He will produce this kind of fruit in you: joy, peace, patience, kindness, goodness, faithfulness. Now the fruit are the personality of the Holy ghost for the saving of your souls. This joy that is spoken of is the joy of this world, but the joy that you receive when you know that you have Christ in your life. And the peace is not the peace of this world but the peace you get knowing that you will get eternal life through Jesus. No worries about whether or not you will make it in because you know for sure that you have given your life to Jesus to control and maintain. Gentleness and self-control are also controlled by the Holy ghost and here there is no conflict with Jewish laws. You won't need to look for honors and popularity, which leads to jealousy and hard feelings. What was the result? Evidently, not good since you are ashamed now even to think about those things you used to do, for all of them ends in eternal hell. Now you are free from the power of sin and are slaves of God. And His benefits to you includes holiness and everlasting life. For the payments of sin is death, the free gift of God is eternal life through Jesus Christ our Lord.

How many of you know that you can have life through the Holy ghost? Some of you are thinking right now that I don't have the Holy ghost and I am still living now, breathing, walking, talking, eating, sleeping, and doing everything that a person who has breath can do. But some of you don't know that without the Holy ghost, you are walking around as a living sinner. Thinking that you will return again with a spiritual body, hoping that you will go to Heaven to be with Jesus. Well, I am here to tell you that you are not going to make it into Heaven unless you get a Spiritual Rebirth and ask God for the Holy ghost, which is the keeper, so you can live now and again. He promised this to us and God does not break His promises. Lots of people have been taught that all you have to do is go to church and don't do anything else but be faithful to the services that is provided for you. This is true in some ways, but you just can't come to church and don't learn or apply any of God's words to your life or obey His laws. There are rules and regulations to serving God. It is a process that we have to go through in order to get to the end of the life span. The bible tells us to let not sin reign in our mortal bodies. The word reign means to control or rule over, be the master of. And the word mortal means subject to death, this body is not going to last always and forever, that you have to give into its sinful desires. Don't give any parts of your bodies to become tools of wickedness, to be used for sinning, but give yourselves completely over to God. You have to allow Jesus to come in and cleanse your bodies from the sins that it was born into. We have the freedom to choose who we want to serve, Jesus or the devil and his angels. Jesus can't come into our bodies and take over unless we allow Him to. We must do the first thing that is required of us to do is to repent. That if we truly and are ready to obey His words. If you want to live in peace and happiness, love on this side, we must repent and stop sinning. The word repent means to turn away from, not always going to the sins but flee from them. God gave commandments to His chosen people and then He grafted us into the will as well, so we all can have the same right as His chosen ones. When He gave the laws and commandments to them, they rejected Him. Doing everything against what He had told them to do. We are trying to serve

Jesus without following the rules and order of human lives. We must obey all the commandments that God have given us. If we do obey all of the laws of God, we will live and have life and have it more abundantly.

God asked them a question, the Israelites, about do they remember how the Lord led them through the wilderness for 40 years. This applies to us as well today, do you remember how Jesus leads you through your trials and tribulations and suffering to make you humble, yes, He humbles you by letting you go hungry, maybe for days at a time. You have to struggle, so you can eat good daily. Testing you to see how you responded to the hunger, or you going to wait on Him or do your own thing to make it happens. Food is for the body, but the word is food for your souls. We are hard headed people acting like the children of Israel, always complaining, not ever satisfied about nothing concerning us. God blesses us and we return back to the things that He has brought us out from. Why, because we don't follow instructions of Jesus to keep us from going back. He always says let me, that word let means to allow Jesus to remove all the things that is not like Him, and the sins that causes the body and soul to lust after. We must allow Him, Jesus, to kill the deeds of the flesh and only He can do it. We can't because when we stop doing the things that are not like Christ sooner or later, we return back to the sins. We cannot keep ourselves from sinning. He said whosoever will let him come, this tells us that it doesn't matter what sin you have done or are in, bring all of your burdens to the Lord and leave them there. I thank Jesus for being a whosoever, I was sinning my way to a burning hell on earth and I knew that there has to be a better way than the way of life that I had chosen for myself. God has a plan and purpose for all of our lives, and we must walk into the plan. Our way of living will not allow us to receive eternal life without going through Jesus.

When we go to the doctors for our illness, he gives us some medicine and pills to take to get better. Sometimes we don't finish or follow-up with the process of getting well. We get a pill from Jesus and feels better, then don't go back for the follow-up. We don't see any needs to continue with the process because we feel better. The pain is gone, so we think that the troubles are over and done with. But if Jesus didn't have an input into the situations, then it will come back with more demons and illness. We believe that Jesus is the Son of God, that's not all of the prescription. We must do a follow-up and complete our mission of health.

Here are some prescription instructions from Doctor Jesus:

- Take a dose of repentance daily to stay away from sins and change one's behavior.

- Confess to Jesus by making known and acknowledging that we are sinners. Call them out with your mouths to God.

- Daily ask forgiveness to be blotted out, ask Jesus to pardon your sins.

- Seek Him daily early in the morning to start off your day.

- Read and study on His words throughout the day to show yourself approval unto God.

- Obey what you have read, submit yourselves to authority.

- Pray and communicate with Jesus, which is personal for you.

- Meditate daily on His words, ponder on them, think about and wait for an answer.

- Fast when necessary to abstain from physical nourishment, food, to achieve a certain level in Christ to help things to be removed from your bodies. To kill the deeds of the flesh.

- Allow and permit Jesus to come into your hearts and cleanse it, so it can be pure.

God's plan is to raise up a nation that will obey His laws and Him only, serve Him with a clean heart. There is a way to God that seen foolish to men. Men didn't make the plans of this world for God. God made the plans in order for men to reign with Him forever. So, there is now no condemnation awaiting those who belongs to Christ Jesus. You are no longer guilty of your sins when you belong to Christ. Once we were under God's curse, doomed forever for our sins. We went alone with the crowd and were just like all the others full of sins. Obeying Satan, the mighty prince of the air and his evil powers. Who is at work right now in the hearts of those who are against the Lord.

All of us used to be just and still is as they are. The people in the bible days were as we are living lives, expressing the evil within us, doing every wicked thing that our passion or evil thoughts might lead us into. God is so rich in mercy, He loves us so much, even thou we were spiritually dead and doomed by our sins, going to hell without a doubt. He made us alive when He raised Jesus from the dead only by His underserving love and favor have we ever been saved. Salvation is not a reward for what we done, so none of us can take any credit for it. It is God Himself who has made us what we are and give us new lives in Him through Christ Jesus.

Long ago God planned that we should spend these lives in helping others. Now don't forget that once we were called heathen and that we were called Godless and unclean by the Jews. They circumcised themselves as a sign of godless. We were enemies of God's children. Back then God had not made a promise for us for we were lost without God's help and hope. But their hearts, too, were still unclean, even though they were going through the ceremonies and rituals of godly. Still disobeyed God's laws, but now we belong to Jesus because of what He's done for you and me with His blood. There was a wall of partition between us, now we are no longer strangers to God and foreigners to heaven. He removes and forgives all sins. For the power of the life-giving spirit and the power is mine through Christ Jesus. He has freed us from the vicious circle of sin and death. Following after the Holy Spirit leads to life and peace in Jesus. Following after the flesh and sins leads to death. The sinful nature within us is against God. It never will obey God's law and it never will.

The first mystery is how do I get rid of sin? The answer is to receive the Holy ghost and then you will be control by the right Spirit. And the only way to receive the Holy ghost is to allow Jesus to come into your life and change and rearrange your minds. Learn of Jesus and His ways and words. Seek out for Jesus, He is waiting on you to call upon Him for help in the world and sinful body. You will have life through the Spirit of Jesus. You will no longer be in the flesh but in the Spirit.

People read the bible and don't see what the words are saying to them or understand the words and parables or mysteries of God. We see through our natural eyes and not our Spiritual eyes, we cannot please God in the flesh. This is where the Holy ghost is needed to do the teaching of God's words. We are blinded and deaf at the words because we don't ask and pray for an understanding. He said in His words that in all of your getting get an understanding. Meaning all of the things that we get in life does not includes an understanding of His words. When you allow

Jesus to change your minds and hearts, then your Spiritual eyes and ears will come open, so you can see and hear the words when they are being taught or read. If you can't see and hear what the words are saying to you, then you don't know how or what you have to do to be saved.

LET'S GO THE UPPER ROOM IN THE BIBLE AND SEE WHO MINDS HAS BEEN CHANGED AND HEARTS FIXED

Acts 2:1-11, seven weeks had passed since Jesus's death and resurrection, and the day of Pentecost had now arrived. The reason I know it was seven weeks is because the annual celebration come 50 days after the Passover ceremonies, when Christ was crucified (see Leviticus 23:16). A mighty wind came and filled the temple where they had their meeting. Then it looked like flames or tongues of fire appeared and settled on their heads. And everyone who was present was filled with the Holy ghost and began speaking in different languages they didn't know or speak before for the Holy Spirit gave them this ability to do so, which was God's Holy Spirit. Many Jews were in Jerusalem that day because of the ceremonies, coming from many different nations. The Jews were amazed to hear their languages being spoken by the disciples who spoke only one language, which was Galileans. They started asking questions, saying that don't all of these disciples speaks Galileans? How is it that they are speaking in our languages from where we were born?

So, do you see what the words are saying? That the Holy ghost came and showed them the power of God. How He can give you different diversity of the Spirit. To carry out His mission to further His kingdom. So, the babbling that men had made up to fool people is a mocker to God's word. They don't know or see this because they are not in the Spirit of God. They know that this is why you can be fooled. They told you that is how you know that they are saved, by speaking in tongues, and you felled for it. Because you can't see the words because of your blindness by the creature and not the creator. That gift that was given to the disciples on that day was because they were going to be teaching and talking to a lot of different nations of people that spoke different languages. In order for God's word to be carried out, they had to be able to communicate with the people in their own languages.

Even though Christ lives within you, your body will die because of sin but your spirit will live for Christ has pardoned or forgave your sins. If you keep on following your sins, you are lost and will perish. But if through the power of the Holy ghost, it kills the evil deeds and you shall enter into God's rest.

You have to admit that you are a sinner, then repent for all of your sins. Seek His face and read His words to get to know Jesus.

CHAPTER 11

What Are Your Must

Growing in God spiritually, this is the process of moving toward maturity in your relationship with God and with other people. Let me tell you what hindrance you to grow. In order to be successful in life and it lasts is that we must give God our lives. We must pray at least three times a day, every day. Read on and see what are our must in this life is in order to have a prosper life on earth today and forever.

- *Lack of knowledge: Acts 18:24-28* - The story about a man named Apollos, an eloquent man and mighty in the scriptures. He was fervent in the spirit, he spoke and taught diligently the things of God. Knowing only the baptism of John, not knowing about Jesus the Redeemer. Out of all of your accomplishments in life will not do you any good without Jesus in the Head and the tail of it.

- *Carnal minded: 1 Corinthians 3:1-3* - You are still baby Christians, controlled by your own desires, not God's. Being jealous of one another divided up into groups. Acting like babes wanting your own way. In fact, you act like people who don't belongs to the Lord at all.

- *Instability: Ephesians 4:14-15* - Then we will no longer be like children, forever changing our minds about what we believe. Someone has told us something different or has cleverly lied to us and made the lie sound like the truth. If we believe the true words of God, we will follow the truth at all times, living truly and become more and more in every way like Christ who is the head of His body which you are using.

- *Dullness: Hebrews 5: 11-14:* See, there is much more that I can teach or say about Jesus or growth, but some people don't seem to listen, so it's hard to make you understand unless you want Him, Jesus, for real. We have been in church and so-called Christians a long time now, but instead we have dropped back to the place where we need someone to teach us all over again. When a person is still living on milk, which is they just started the words, it shows that he or she isn't very far long in the life of Christ. And doesn't know much about the difference between right or wrong. This person is not ready for solid Spiritual Words. Once you have tasted and felt the mighty powers of the world to come, then you will seek out your musts.

When you became of age, you weren't taught that you now have some must that you have to attend to. Since you became so-called grown, you still didn't know your must. The bible says that "when I was a child, I spoke as a child, I did childish things. But now that I became a man, I put away childish things, now I have some must I must follow in order to live out the rest of my life. You are chosen by God and hired by God. Now you have some MUST that you have to do in order to work on His job or in His vineyard. You are chosen to do the work for the Master, called out to be a witness. The decisions are God's decisions, His choice, His picks, whom He wants. Do you know what are your must? A lot of us don't know what are our must. What I mean about that is that we know what we think we want and are supposed to be doing or having in this life. But do you really know what are your must? First of all, you must walk in three things everyday of your life: in Christ, in the Scriptures, and the last is in prayer.

You Musts:

- Make sure, absolutely sure, that you are a new creation in Christ Jesus. A new creature, men or women.

- Flee from youthful lusts, still doing things of the flesh as though you are a child or baby.

- Constantly examine yourself, making sure you continue in the faith of Christ.

- Seek first the kingdom of God and His righteousness.

- Live a crucified life in Christ, a life of self-denial and sacrifice. Letting go of this world, not adhering to the deeds of the flesh. Been reborn again to gain eternal life.

- Study and obey the scriptures daily.

- Live by the Word of God and proclaim it. Let the words of God live down on the inside of you.

- Pray daily as Christ has taught you how to pray in the Lord's prayer. Praying for the church, the whole world for all people everywhere, pray for laborers moment by moment, striving to gain an unbroken consciousness of the Lord.

- Take some extended time for fervent prayer when special needs exist.

- Must be willing to give his or her loyalty to the Lord.

- Must be willing to follow all of the instructions of the Holy ghost's guidance. Willing to go the extra mile that is required to get God's work done.

- Must be humble, be a person of fasting and prayer.

- Be a person of repentance and not be a person of gossip, talebearing, or a judgmental critic.

This is Paul speaking to the Ephesians church and to us as well. Saying that he who is a prisoner for the Lord. Meaning you can't get away when the Lord has chosen or called you to do His will. You will get caught by God before you leave this earth. You can change your move, change your name, even dye your hair. You still have an arrest warrant over your head. That you must get served by Jesus. Paul is saying now that I have been served here in jail for serving the Lord; to live and act in a way worthy of those who have been chosen for such wonderful blessings as these.

The second verse takes me back to a lesson that we had in bible class one Wednesday night. The Beatitudes of Jesus in Matthew 5: 3-12, when He was preaching and teaching on the Mount. Jesus said these words, "Blessed are the poor in spirit, for theirs is the ding dim of heaven. Blessed are they that mourn, blessed are the meek, blessed are they, which do hunger and thirst after righteousness; for they shall be filled."

Be humble and gentle, be patient with each other, forbearing one another in love. Showing that I can wait on the Lord to bring you to the place that He has brought me. Not always getting upset about your faults because of my love that I have for Jesus. Endeavoring, meaning striving to achieve or reach the togetherness by the Holy Spirit in the bond of peace. See, we must come together, unity is one. This is not a two-way religion, we must come together soon and very soon. Now I have got where I need to be in the Lord daily, but I can't handle that you haven't made it yet. We are supposed to pray for one another to make it in the realm of God.

There is one body, and we are all part of that body. We need each other's. I can't make up my mind to serve God and stop dealing with you because you haven't made up your minds. Get saved and only deal with the ones that are saved because He saved me first. This is not how we are supposed to act or be in Jesus. We have the same Spirit, and we all have been called to the same glorious future.

For there is only one Lord, one faith, and one baptism. Any other is not of God but gods. One owner, one CEO, one boss, one job but several positions. You know when we get a great job, we have certain people that we tell about the job. Sometimes we don't tell no one because we want to keep it for ourselves. But at Jesus' job sites, it will take for us to tell someone how they can get on. We need them to help make up the body of Christ, God wants us to have patience and allow Him to teach and bring others up to speed. We will say this, I don't want to work or be with her or him to help them because they don't know how to act. Or they haven't got Jesus yet. And I am saved, so I can't deal with them.

We all have the same God who is over us all and in us all, and God is living through every part of us. He has given each one of us a special ability to do His will; what if all of us was preachers, or singers, there would be no need for anybody else to be here. He could have just created one person to do everything on the job of His work site. God has a rich storehouse of gifts to get His job done. You can't cross a sea by merely staring into the water. Exhausting yourself to fight against the flowing and powerful current, just go with the flow. Actions speaks louder than words, remind yourself of God's love for you and then the negative emotions will flee.

The Psalmist tells us that when Jesus returned triumphantly to Heaven after His resurrection and victory over Satan, He gave generous gifts to men. Not one woman or man but to all men, all of us. So, you see that you have must in life. We have to be qualified and equipped to do His works, you must have life's experiences to do His will. He has given us the necessary tools to work in His vineyards. Some apostles and some prophets, some evangelists, and so forth. It takes all of us to make up the body of Christ. It is God that will equip us and train us or give us the skills to work. Until we all believe in Jesus about our salvations and about our Savior, who is God's Son Jesus and all become grown in the Lord to the place of being perfect in Christ, then and only then we will no longer be like children forever changing our minds about what to do or how to act and whom to serve. Someone told us something different or cleverly lied to us and made the lie sound like the truth about how to come and receive and Jesus as the head of our lives. God doesn't want us to live any longer as the unsaved people do. For they are all blinded and confused, also deaf their close hearts are full of darkness. Sinners are far away from the life of Christ, they have shut their minds against Him. They cannot understand His ways and plans. Don't care about the right and the wrong, given themselves over to impure ways being driven by their evil minds and lusts of the flesh.

This isn't the way that Jesus taught us, you heard His voice and learned from Him the truths concerning Himself. So, throw off your old and evil ways that is rotten through and through, full of lust and shame and come to Christ Jesus. Now your attitudes and thoughts must be constantly changing for the better you. You must be a new and different person, holy and clean for Jesus. Stop lying to each other and tell the truth, whether it hurts or not. Nursing the grudge of others, allowing the sun to go down on your anger. Because when you are angry, you give a mighty foothold to the devil and his angels. Using bad languages, being mean, bad tempered, quarreling, harsh words, and dislike of each other. This should have no place in your lives. Instead be kind to each other, tendered hearted, forgiving one another just as Christ has given us because we belong to God.

CHAPTER 12

Watch Them Dogs

WHO IN THE HELL LEFT THE GATE OPEN?

DOG - Canine mammal - A domestic, carnivorous animal with a long muzzle, a fur coat, and a long fur-covered tail, whose characteristic call is a bark (Ruff). The word mammal means warm-blooded vertebrate animals; a class of warm-blooded vertebrate animals that have in the female milk, secreting organs for feeding the young. The class includes human beings, apes, many four-legged animals, whales, dolphins, and bats. The word canine means tooth point between the incisors and the first bicuspids. Most mammals have two in each jaw, the incisors are flat, sharp front tooth. Used for cutting and tearing of food. The bicuspids is a tooth with two points that come between the canines and the molar in the adult human's mouth.

The bible talks bout and tell us of the different kinds of dogs that we are or are acting like.

The different kinds of dog in the bible that we are or portray:

- *Hypocrite - Matt. 7:6* - Judging others, criticizing, and trying to cast out beams out of everyone else's, eyes except your own eyes.

- *Carnivorous - 1 King 14:11 -* Flesh eating dogs. Always biting off more than you can chew. Destroying the looks of the flesh of others.

- *Blood eating - 1 King 21:19 -* Licking blood that has been shed. Pouring salt in other people's wounds. Searching to lick up the blood that has been shed by someone just to get you a taste of it.

- *Dangerous - Psalms 22:16 -* Enemy, circle around you for evil; acting evil toward someone. Or doing evil, telling your business to hurt you or destroy you.

- *Domesticated - Matt. 15:26-27 -* Eating with unwashed hands. Want the good things in life but don't want to work to achieve them.

- *Unclean - Isaiah 66:3 -* Impurity, choose your own ways of life and not the way of God. Do exactly what the Lord tells us not to do.

- *Promiscuity - Deut. 23:18 -* Undiscriminating sexual behaviors, prostituting your bodies, sleeping with several people for money, fornicating yourselves to please the flesh.

- *Contempt - 1 Sam. 17:43 -* Treating people like they are inhuman. Not having or showing love for your fellowman.

- *Worthlessness - 2 Sam. 9:8 -* Having no value, no goods, usefulness. Not doing anything or achieving any goals that you set in your life.

- *Satan - Psalms 22:20 -* The enemy of God, the Lord of evil powers. Acting and protruding as the devil. Not obeying God's commandments or doing His wills.

- *Gentiles - Matt. 15:26 -* Wanting to get the Holy Ghost without being cleaned. Wanting God to come in with the filth and dirt of your souls.

- *False Teachers - 2 Peter 2:22 -* Learned and know the truth and not living it. Going on with your sins and you know what you are teaching is for you first. Not teaching false documents but know what the words are saying and not living it. Not being convicted yourselves first, false teachers are like dogs that goes back to what he has vomited and also like pigs washed only to come back and wallow in the mud again. This is the way it is with those who turns again to their sins after having been washed by Jesus.

- *The Unsaved - Revelations 22:15* - Strayed away from God, was giving Him a life but turned back into the world because you got mad.

DIFFERENT TYPES OF DOGS:

They are determined, persistent, strong willed, strong minded, gritty, and steadfast.

- *Pit Bull Terrier* - A large but muscular and powerful dog. Bit down on something or someone and it is hard to release that dog. That's the way some of us are, bit down on hate and it is hard to release it. A Pit Bull is quiet, he just looks and watches for a chance to strike.

- *Doberman Pinscher* - This is another large dog with medium size. He is powerful with a smooth black or dark brown coat, often used as a guard dog. Sitting, watching, guarding the wrong things, waiting for a chance to strike. Taking upon itself to watch what he wants to watch to find fault to strike.

- *German Shepherd* - He is another large dog with medium length hair. Has pointed ears and a muscular build. Makes a lot of noise, always barking and running his mouth at birds, bugs, or whatever he hears or sees. Barking all the time and ain't going to do nothing.

- *Rottweiler* - A large, big headed dog, slick, powerful. Doubled jawed, watches you from the corner of his eyes. Don't care who or whom he bites. Sometimes will turn on the one who has taken care of him. That's the way some of us are, we will help you get a person and then turn on you for no apparent reason. Because it is in their nature.

- *Poodle* - Curly haired dog, some large and some small with thick coats of curly hair. Wants to be groomed and fed and taken care of. Just lay around wasting time, waiting on you to do for them. Carry and pet them, washing and grooming, then sits on a pedalstool to be loved. They are useless to you, you spend your money on them and they don't protect or guard you or your belongings. The small dogs, Tea Cups, Pomeranians, dogs are dogs, you just can hold in your hands for show.

In your bibles, the book of Philippians 3:1-4 where Paul speaks to us and what he is saying is that whatever happens, dear friends, be glad in the Lord. He said that he never gets tired of telling us this and it is good for us to hear it again and again. To watch out for those wicked men or dangerous dogs who say you must be circumcised to be saved. For it isn't the cutting of our bodies that makes us children of God, it is worshipping Him with our spirits in truth. That is the only true circumcision, we as Christians glory in what Jesus has done for us and realize that we are helpless to save ourselves. Yet if anyone ever had reason to hope that he could save himself, it would be Paul. If others could be saved by what they are, certainly he could. Paul went through the Jewish initiation ceremony when he was eight-days-old; he was born into a pure blooded Jewish home that was a Benjamin family. He was a real Jew a member of the Pharisees who demand the strictest obedience to every Jewish law and custom with sincere. So much that he greatly persecuted the churches and he tried to obey every Jewish rule and regulations.

Verse 7 in Philippians 3rd chapter says all of these things that we counted as worthwhile are useless to God and our souls. Come from among those things, so you can put your trust in Christ alone. Yes, everything is worthless and vain when it's compared with the priceless gain of knowing Christ Jesus my Lord. Put aside all else counting it worthless than nothing, in order that you can have Christ and become one with Him. No longer counting on being saved by being good enough or by obeying God's laws. By trusting Christ to save you for God's way of making us right with Himself depends on faith counting on Christ alone.

Now give up everything else and try to find it to be the only way to really know Jesus. To experience the mighty power that brought him back to life again and find out what it means to suffer and to die with

Him. So, whatever it takes, I will be one who lives in the fresh newness of life of those who are alive from the dead. Paul is not calling himself perfect until he reaches perfection in Jesus, he says that he has not learned all that he should yet. But he keeps working toward that day when he will finally be all that Christ saved him for and wants him to be. Jesus wants us to strain to reach the end of the race and receive the gift of the Holy ghost for which God is calling us up to Heaven because of what Jesus did for us.

Watch out for yourselves to make sure that you are not being one of these dogs in this world because no dog goes to heaven.

My number one life law is you either get it or you don't. I can tell you that while it has taken me 30 to 40 something odd years to get it. You, on the other hand, might not have that length of time on earth to get it right with Jesus. Time has been shortened for the elite ones, you might say that we are in the flesh and young, so our flesh calls for everything that is not like Jesus. This is where you have to ask Jesus to kill the deeds of the flesh and renew a right spirit within you. To know the rules of life is to read your bibles and learn of Him Jesus to gain eternal life with Him. To drift is to be in hell, to be in heaven is to steer your life to Christ Jesus. We create our own experience in life, you cannot change what you don't acknowledge. Life rewards actions, life is managed, it is not cured. There is power in forgiveness you have to name before you can claim it. Let's just be honest, we want to run things and be independent and all grown up, but the real truth of the matter is it hasn't been more than two or three years since we were playing with toys in the same room we now want to make out in. Not too long ago we were fantasizing about children things we used to do or wanted to do. You have the tools to make the right choices to get the results that you want.

There are 10 Losers Laws of Life:

1. just make it up as you go along (there are no rules you can live by).

2. it is written in the stars (for $4.95 per minute, you can hear about your future).

3. the devil made me do it (how to ignore the things that really make you tick).

4. denial really is a river in Egypt (how to avoid change by avoiding your problems).

5. be patient; life will eventually deliver (how to look out the window and hope it comes your way).

6. life is what it is (how to accept what you don't want).

7. get it right once and you are home free (how to coast from the top of the hill).

8. people are what they are (how to accept crummy relationships).

9. get even through grudges (you are just mad and there is nothing anyone can do about it).

10. live lucky (how to sit on the shore and hope that your ship comes in).

Start thinking about what you want in this life, and I hope and pray that you choose Jesus as your head and leader to guide you to life's success. Don't be named once among you as being one of those dogs.

CHAPTER 13

A Call to Perserverance

This word, perseverance, means in doing something despite the difficulty or delay in achieving success.

The 3rd Sunday in July on the 20th day in the year of 2010, Dr. Luzine Davis taught us to separate ourselves and come out from sin. Give God a life, allow Him to save us to live in perfection in Jesus, she said that Jesus is warning us through His words. Matthews is the teaching of Jesus and maybe you will believe what He is saying to us in Matthews 24 chapter to His disciples then and today, 2019. He was leaving the grounds of the temple, His disciples came along with Him, they were pointing out the different temple buildings. Jesus told them that all of those buildings will be knocked down with no one stone left on top of another. They wanted to know when this will happen? But while they were sitting on the slopes of Mt. Olives, they asked several questions concerning when will this happen and what event will happen to show us your return and the end of the world. Jesus was letting them know that when He has been crucified, the way things was going on in the world of ministry will be changed. The temples that men built to worship and control people in will be torn down. The very day that He was crucified, the temple was rented and came down. We don't have to have a priest to go to God for us, we can seek and serve Him without anyone else going to Jesus for us. We can ask for forgiveness for our self. Don't let anyone fool you that word deceive means to mislead, trick, or fool. He said that "many will come claiming to be the Messiah and will lead many of you astray." Just because you hear of wars beginning and rumors of wars, this is not a sign of my Jesus coming or His return. Jesus also said that "this must happen or come to past, but the end is not yet. No one knows the day or the hour when He will return for His saints. We just have to be ready while the blood is still running warm in our veins. The nations and kingdom of the earth will rise up against each other and there will be famines and earthquakes in many places. This is only the beginning of the horror of times, sad days, and sorrowful days. Now if you are a child of God, you will be hated, tortured and killed because you belong to God. But you must remember that man cannot kill the souls, only the flesh. Many of you will fall back into the world of sins and betray each other and hate each other because you haven't received the gift of the Holy ghost, which is the keeper. We have to stand and see the salvation of the Lord. The Comforter, which is the Holy ghost, will keep you from being scared and you will be able to go through your suffering while following Christ Jesus. He that stay steadfast, unmovable, always abiding in the words of God will be saved.

Now learn a lesson or pay attention to the fig trees or any tree. Notice the signs of time through the seasons of the years. When the branches are tender and the leaves begin to sprout, you know that summer is almost here. Just like you know when the season changes, you are to know that your time is near the return of Christ is at the door of your life. Then at last, this age will come to its close. God is not a lying God, all of these things will come to past before His words fall. He is coming back and His words says He is coming, that we must be ready going to our dressing room and getting dressed for the bride and groom.

He warns us by the lightening, the thunder, by the way people are acting or treating you because love has gross cold. Do you remember when the world got at ease, in a comfort zone? Everybody was partying, having banquets and weddings. Having a reason to drink and be merry, laid back, getting high on whatever their high was. They were doing the same thing that was happening in the days of Noah. God told Noah to tell the people to repent and turn away from their sins. God was going to destroy the people from the earth. We are like that today, not believing what the servants and prophets are telling us today. God saw that the wickedness of men was so great on the earth, being evil, not loving one another, not giving our lives to Christ so we can be spared. (Genesis 6 & 7) Jesus is letting us know that God will destroy us if we continually sin and reject Him. He told Noah to make an ark, but while Noah was obeying God's order, the people were laughing, pointing, and talking about how he has lost his mind. God told him how to make it and what to use to build the foundation of the ark. He used gopher wood and made rooms in the ark. People will talk about you whether you are obeying God, doing exactly what He told you to do. Just because you decided to follow Jesus and obey His will by living a saved life, they will talk about you, do you care? No, they are blinded to the truth of Jesus. He's coming like a thief in the night or day, so you better get persistent in getting Jesus in your life. The only safety zone is in Jesus when He shut up the doors and says it's too late. When Gabriel blows his trumpet and Jesus puts one leg on the land and one on the sea, it will be too late to seek or search for Jesus. So, come on in out of the storm and rain, run for cover in Christ Jesus because your end is near. A leader or servant of God should be Holy. (1 Peter 2:5) God is a holy God, He said holy without no man shall see the Lord (Hebrews 12:14). Noah was acting with perseverance in his spirit and soul. Determine to do as God had instructed him to do without giving up, no matter what was the consequences.

Needeth not to be ashamed, rightly dividing the word of truth. (2 Timothy 2:15) God is the only approval that you need when serving or learning of Him. When you read your words and see what they are saying to you, then whatever you do in the Lord will be alright and good. Not be ashamed of what the Spirit has told or showed you to do or say concerning Jesus. Wherefore, holy brethren and sisters, partakers of the heavenly calling, consider the Apostle and High Priest of our profession, Christ Jesus (Hebrews 3:1). For the gifts and calling of God are without repentance (Romans 11:29). You don't have to be saved to answer your call or do His will. Jesus is calling for the sinners, lost, and unlearned ones in this world to do His will. He gifted us before we were born or you to live perfect and complete in Him. 1 Thessalonians 4:7 says for God hath not called us unto uncleanness but unto holiness. He will give you a spiritual rebirth and wash you clean to do His will.

Daniel 3 chapter tells a story about a king named Nebuchadnezzar, he made a golden statue, which stood 90-feet high and nine-feet wide to sit up on the Plain of Dura in the province of Babylon. One day he was having a dedication of his statue and he sent invitations to all the princes, governors, captains, judges, treasures, counselors, and sheriffs of all of his empire. When they had all arrived and were standing before the monument, a herald shouted out, "O, people of all nations and languages, this is the King's command. When the King Nebuchadnezzar's golden statue. Anyone who refuses to obey will immediately be thrown into a flaming furnace." So, when the band started playing, everyone, whatever nation, language, or religion, was to falling to the ground and worshiped the statue. But some of the officials went to the King and accused some of the Jews of refusing to worship the golden statue. The Jews who refused to worship was Shadrach, Meshach, and Abednego, who was put in charge of Babylonian affairs. They refuse to serve the King's gods or to worship the golden statue that the King set-up. The King called them into him and gave them another chance to worship the golden statue. They refused the offer and said their very words to the King, "We are not worried about what will happen to us. If we are thrown into the flaming furnace, our God is able to have and know without a shadow of doubt and are very persistent that God will deliver you on time or out of the hands of the enemies." There ain't no buts about if He will or I hope He will. It's about knowing that He will trusting in Him and having faith that He will do just what He say. When they said if it be so, they were simply saying if it be His will. Our God, naming and claiming God as their personal Savior. Then they went on to say whom we serve. See that makes a difference to say that you serve Him and to truly and really serve Him. Look at their two small words, knowing what God can do and without doubting what God can do. He is able to deliver us from the burning fiery furnace. The word Able is strong and powerful, this means that He can do it. Deliver is the word that was also used in their saying, which is present, getting you out, bringing forth or changing the way it was to a new way. Releasing the strong hold, so you can pin point where and what or who wants to be delivered from. They said out of thine hand, o, King. The next verse in the 3rd chapter said, "But if not, meaning if it's not His will, let it be known, tell everybody this that we will not serve thy gods, nor worship the golden image which thou hast set up. See the devil will set you up and fool you to believe that this is right, or the right way to go."

CHAPTER 14

This World is Not My Home

God the Father chosen you long ago before you were born. Not to get to comfortable in this world, this world is not your home. We are just pilgrims traveling through this borrow land. The Holy Spirit has been at work in your hearts, cleansing you with the blood of Jesus so that you can please Him, Jesus. Jesus can bless you richly and grant you with the increasing freedom from all anxiety and fear of dying without being saved.

I press toward the mark for the prize of the high calling of God in Christ Jesus. (Phil. 3:14) This is a faithful saying, and these things I will that thou affirm constantly, that they which have believed in God might be careful to maintain good works. These things are good and profitable unto men. (Titus 3:8) We as little children of God has to keep on striving to be the best in Christ that we can be. Do all that it is to do to obtain our place in the mansion of God. Jesus said in my father's house are many mansions, and if it were not so, I would have told you. There are rooms in God's kingdom for us, this walk in the world is temporary and will not last for eternity. Heaven is my goal and should be yours, too, who reach perfection in Jesus Christ our Lord.

The unrighteousness shall not inherit the kingdom of God. What? Know ye not that your bodies are the temple of the Holy ghost, which is a gift that Jesus wants to give you, which is of God and ye are not your own. For we were brought with a price; therefore glorify God in your bodies and your spirits and minds which are God's. Forasmuch as ye know that you were not redeemed with corruptible things, as silver and gold. From your vain conversation received by tradition from your fathers but with the precious blood of Christ as of a lamb without blemish and without spot. Use every parts of your body to give glory back to God because He owns it. Jesus was fore ordained before the foundation of the world but was manifest in these last times for us. Being born again, not of corruptible seed but of incorruptible by the word of God which liveth and abideth for ever. For you to have a new life in Jesus was not passed on to you from your parents, for the life they gave you will fade away and your soul has to have a resting place until Jesus' return. For all flesh is as grass, and all the glory of man as the flower of the grass. The grass withered, and the flowers thereof falleth away. All of our greatness is like a flower that droops and falls. But the words of the Lord endureth forever, and this is the words which by the gospel is preached unto you daily everywhere. God's Words will last forever and His messages are the good news that is preached to you. Wherefore laying aside come out from among those things and people that are going in the directions of Christ. Stop acting like your bodies belong to you and this is your home here on earth. You still have a chance to be in the right standards and perfect will of God. Every time your sun rises, which is your eyes and your tongues are not glued to the top of your mouths, you still have a little time to see Jesus and give your life to Him to be perfectly saved for His will and kingdom to go home, to partake of His righteousness and His glory.

God has to draw near to you, and He is calling you everyday of your life through sickness, death, storm and the rain, pain, sufferings, and the trails of this life.

We are thieves and murderers killing the body and souls like the body belongs to you with the evil and sins of this world. Consuming all of this worldly stuff upon your bodies like your soul will die with your bodies, but it will not. Our souls live forever and we have that choice to decide where or with whom we want our souls to live. Allowing Jesus to do in your life what He needs to do to make you complete and perfect for the

Kingdom of God. Asking the Holy ghost to keep you on the right path, so you want fall or slip into diver's places and things of this world. God said that if you are of the world and love the things of this world that are evil, then you are not His and don't belongs to Him. You want to go home where you belong, to Jesus, holy and perfect.

You are a fool to think that you do have a place with Him, Jesus, when you live an evil and sinful life for the rest of your lives. During such things as worshipping idol gods, committing adulterers, prostituting your bodies, men laying with men, women laying with women will not have a place of rest in God. Neither will anyone who steals, rod, or is very greedy for the things of this world and other materialized items will not have a place in God's kingdom for your souls. Being drunkard with wine, always causing confusion with others will not inherit the kingdom of God. When we are born again saints, we are set apart from this unrighteousness, set apart to do His will and obey His laws for the home to come which is heaven. The bible says that sin will not enter in (Revelation 21:27).

Being brought under the power of sin is a sure ticket and in heritage to HELL. Isaiah 64:6 tells us that we are all like an unclean thing, and all our righteousness are like filthy rags. For they being ignorant of God's righteousness and seeking to establish their own righteousness have not submitted to the righteousness of God. God made Jesus who knew no sins to be guilty of sins for us that we might become righteousness of God in Him. For the wrath of men does not produce the righteousness of God to enter in.

The things that I asked God for:

- I asked God for strength that I might achieve, but I was made weak that I might learn to be humble and obey His words.

- I asked for health that I might do greater things, I was given infirmity that I might pray always and appreciate life.

- I asked for riches that I might be happy and without debts. I was given poverty that I may be grateful and wise.

WOULDN'T MIND DYING, IF DYING WAS ALL

- I asked for power that I might have the praise of men. I was given weakness that I would know and feel the needs of God.

- I asked for all things that I might enjoy life. But I was given life in Jesus that I might enjoy all things. I got nothing that I asked for but everything that I had hope for. Almost despite myself, my unspoken prayers were answered. I am among all most richly blessed!

King David was a man that prayed to God whenever he was in turmoil or distress. He asked God to hear his prayer, O, Lord, recognizing that Jesus is the King of Kings and Lord of Lord. He also asked him to give ear to his supplications. See, we think that God answers our prayers, yes, He does when we are sincere with ourselves and Him. Jesus judges our hearts and our hearts let Him know when we are real with Him. Then David knew that God is a faithful God. He is faithful to His promises to us, Jesus promised us that if we give Him our life, allow Him to lead and guide us through this life on earth that we can be with Him forever in His heavenly home. Also, that He will supply all of our needs according to His riches and glory. Anything that we need or want in this life, Jesus will give it to us. Whether it be big or small, this is personal with God to have a relationship with Him. You must get to know Jesus for yourself, take time out of your busy life and learn of Him. We were taught and been mislead about God. We were taught that we are saved and going to heaven, as long as we believe that Jesus Christ is the Son of God. That sounded too easy to me to be true. Well, it is more than just a belief in Christ. See, we have been here before, at funerals, the death of our loved ones, and the sad thing is that when we die in our sins, we will go to hell. We even tell ourselves that we will give Jesus some time when I stop doing what the world is doing. But you will not make it to Jesus trying to right yourself or change your life yourself. Trying to stop doing things against your bodies that causes habits to be formed. Sleeping with the enemies and not married, telling lies and going against each other. Jesus wants us to come just as we are, whatever sins that we are enduring. Allow Jesus to forgive, remove, destroy, and reborn us again to Him, so we can go home to heaven to live in paradise with our Heavenly Father God. We don't have to wait to die to live in heaven, we can have a piece of heaven right here on earth.

Satan's job is to kill, steal, and destroy you while the blood is running warm in your bodies. He was here from the beginning of time when God said let us go down and make man, Satan came down, too, with his hosts of demon angels. His job will accomplish all what he was made to do if you allow him. He will destroy your rights, steal your joy, and kill your vessels that God had made for Himself. Our whole body belongs to God. For the devil has persecuted our souls, yes, he has chased you and caught you to live for him. To do his will against God's will. Jesus is waiting on you to come to him just like you are. Crying out I once was lost, but now I am found, blind but now I see, and deaf but now I can hear what Jesus is saying to me, for me to live and have life and have it more abundantly.

Back to King David's story is that he only called and prayed for God when he was feeling low and depressed. So, when he did pray while he was in such suffering, God came and blessed his soul where he didn't feel down and out long. But God wants us to pray and called upon Him for everything in life that we go through, whether it be good or bad, happy or sad. Try Jesus and then you can be a witness of this little book about wouldn't mind dying if dying was all, God said what?

Have you read the book of life's instruction? BIBLE, basic instructions before leaving earth. You don't have to figure it out because God has already worked it out for you and me. A lot of us right now are depressed about the cares of this world. This world is not our home, we are just passing by, we have a heavenly home to go to. I am asking you to come to Jesus while there is still day light in your souls because when it gets dark, no man can work.

ONE SOLITARY LIFE (WHICH WAS JESUS)
AUTHOR UNKNOWN

He was born in an obscure village, the child of a peasant woman, he grew up in still another village, where he worked in a carpenter shop until he was 30. Then for three years, he was an itinerant preacher.

He never wrote a book.

He never held an office.

He never had a family or owned a house.

He didn't go to college.

He never traveled 200 miles from the place where he was born. He did none of these things one usually associates with greatness.

He had no credentials but himself.

He was only 33 when public opinion turned against him.

His friends ran away. He turned over to his enemies and went through the mockery of a trial. He was nailed to a cross between two thieves.

When he was dying, his executioners gambled for his clothing, the only property he had on earth. When he was dead, he was laid in a borrowed grave through the pity of a friend.

Nineteen centuries have come and gone, and today, he is the central figure of the human race, the leader of mankind's progress.

All the armies that ever marched, all the navies that ever sailed, all the parliaments that ever sat, all the kings that ever reigned, put together, have not affected the life of men on earth as much as that one solitary life Jesus.

CHAPTER 15

Spiritual Gifts

Both spiritual gifts and natural talents must be employed in the power of the Holy Ghost and the Holy Spirit, not in the self-energy of the flesh in order to please God and bring positive results.

There are various spiritual gifts that are listed in the book of Romans 12, Ephesians 4, and 1 Corinthians 13-15 and elsewhere in the bible. The gifts are divided into teaching/leadership, service and gifts given to authenticate the of apostles and prophets, particularly at the beginning of a new age when God does something new and different in the world.

Here is a rather complete list:

Apostle, Prophet, Evangelist, Pastor-teacher, Administration, Leadership, Faith, Knowledge, Wisdom, Exhortation, Discernment, Ministering, Service, Giving, Tongues, Interpretation of Tongues, Miracles, Healings, Mercy, Hospitality.

Now there are varieties of gifts but the same Spirit, and there are varieties of service but the same Lord Jesus Christ, and there are varieties of working but it is the same God, the Father who inspires them all in everyone. To each is given the manifestation of the Spirit for the common good. Let's go back and explain the different gifts in details.

Apostle (apostolos) the Greek word means one sent forth (on an official errand).

Prophet, prophecy (prophetes), lit: to speak forth, to proclaim the mind and counsel of God.

Evangelist, evangelism (evangelistes). from eu=well, plus angelos = messenger, the gift of bringing the good news of God to unbelievers individually and in groups.

Faith, the ability to believe God for new direction and power visionary faith that sets in motion events others can join in and follow.

Knowledge. Systematic understanding of truth in broad, sweeping terms, so that others may be trained and instructed. Some may be given the gift to teach and edify the body.

Wisdom, the ability to make wise choices and decisions at critical forks in the road.

Exhortation, encouragement (paraklesis). To call alongside, comfort, strengthen, to counsel, exhort, bring aid, admonish. The same Greek word describes the Holy ghost's role in our lives.

Discernment (of spirits) is a gift to judge or evaluate the spirits, so as to distinguish whether something is from God or from an evil source. More reliable and consistent.

Ministering, to serve. A wide variety of activities one performs with the help of God to comfort, encourage, support and build up God's people.

Service (help), to lay hold of (and support), especially the weak and needy. To minister to others and meet their needs.

Giving is the gift of sharing and imparting, not only money but other resources. Some are given the gift of giving, so they can act as stewards over material resources in the body of Christ.

Tongues (that is, "kinds of languages"). The ability to speak in other languages not previously learned but known languages to men. The gift is for the purpose of praising God. It must be directed to God, not to be used to pass a message from one member to another or from one member to the congregation. A sign to unbelievers.

Interpretation of Tongues. The ability to translate unknown languages, so as to edify the instruct others regarding what has been said.

Miracles. The ability to raise men from the dead, call fire down from heaven and otherwise present signs that authenticate the power of God in certain situations.

Healing(s). Ability to heal at the physical, emotional, and spiritual levels. The word is plural in Greek, probably suggesting that the ability to heal refers to all three levels of man. Today, God sometimes heals physically but more often emotionally and spiritually. A valuable gift for a counselor.

Mercy (eleos). An ability to touch inwardly with compassion. To be exercised with cheerfulness.

Hospitality. Love of strangers. May not be a spiritual gift but definitely a Christian virtue. All believers are to practice hospitality.

A Christian's service involves the entire trinity.

1. The gifts of the Holy ghost are the sovereign choice of the Holy Spirit.

2. The place of our service is chosen by the Son of God, Jesus.

3. The working, or style, of our ministry is determined by the Father, God.

The bible verses in 1 Corinthains 12:5-7 tells us that now there are varieties of gifts but the same Spirit and there are varieties of service but the same Lord Jesus Christ and there are varieties of working, but it is the same God, the Father who inspires them all in everyone. To each is given the manifestation of the Spirit for the common good.

God has a standard of requirements; Colosians 3:10 says and have put on the new man, which is renewed in knowledge after the image of Him that created Him. Meaning that we must be reborn in order to successfully do God's will and be more affected in His works. Receiving the gift of the Holy ghost, which is God's personality, attitude, and character of the created God, which are the nine fruit of the Spirit of God. God's plan is to raise up a nation that will obey His laws and order. Serve Him and Him only. There is a way to God that seem foolish to men. But men didn't make the plans for God, God made the plans for men in order to reign with Him forever. (Romans 8: 1-13) So, there is now no condemnation awaiting those who belongs to Christ Jesus. You are no longer guilty of your sins when you belong to Jesus, He removes and forgives all sins. For the power of the life-giving spirit and this power of this power is mine through Christ Jesus. Has freed me from vicious circle of sin and death. We aren't saved from sin's grasp by knowing the commandments of God because we can't and don't keep them. But God put into effect a different plan to save us. He sent His own Son in a human body like ours, except that ours are sinful and destroyed sin's control over us by giving Himself as a sacrifice for our sins. So now we can obey God's laws if we follow after the Holy Spirit and no longer obey the old evil nature within us. Those who let themselves be controlled by their lower natures live only to please themselves, but those who follow after the Holy ghost find themselves doing the things that are pleasing to God. Following after the Holy ghost leads to life and peace, but following after the old man leads to death. Because the old man's sinful nature within us is against God. It never did obey God's laws and never will. That's why those who are still under the control of their old sinful selves bent on following their old evil desires can never pleases God.

When you receive the Holy ghost, then you will be controlled by the right spirit. So, you can keep God's laws and live in heaven right here on earth and not be found guilty. In order to please God is to receive the gift of the Holy ghost and then you will no longer be in flesh but under the Spirit. People read the bible and don't see exactly what the words are saying, there are mysteries and revelations in the words of God. Most of them believe in what they read and not what the words are actually saying to them. They see through natural eyes and ears, not spiritual eyes and ears, still in the flesh trying to please God. You have to be spiritually reborn and saved to see the laws of God spiritually. If you cannot see what the words are saying, then it is impossible for you to know how or what the word of God wants you to know and how to live in order to receive Him and eternal life with Him. When you have a changed mind and heart, then your spiritual eyes and ears will come open and in turn you can see the truth and know what to do to be saved.

Example: Let's go to the upper room in the bible and see who's minds have been changed and hearts are fixed.

ACTS 2:1-11

1st verse says that seven weeks had passed since Jesus's death and resurrection and the day of Pentecost had now arrived. The reason that I know it was seven weeks is the annual celebration comes 50 days after the Passover ceremonies when Jesus Christ was crucified. You can find that in Leviticus 23:16.

Second verse said that a mighty wind came and filled the temple where they had their meetings. People used to come together and reason together and learn.

Third verse continues to say then it looked like flames or tongues of fire appeared and settled on their heads. Because of their actions and the way they were acting.

Fourth verse tells us that everyone who was present was filled with the HOLY GHOST and began speaking in languages they didn't know, for the Holy Spirit which is God gave them this ability. They spoke in languages that they didn't know how to speak in at first. Many Jews were in Jerusalem that day because of the ceremonies, they came from different nations. The Jews were amazed to hear their languages being spoken by the disciples who only spoken one language, which was Galileans. "Don't all of these disciples speak Galilean?" asked by the Jews who were astounded and amazed of what they were hearing. Then they wanted to know how is it that they the disciples are able to speak in our languages from where we were born?

So, do you see what the words are saying to us? That the Holy ghost came and showed them the power of God. How He can give you different and diversity of the Spirit. To carry out His missions to further His kingdom. So, the babbling and the learned tongues that men had made up to fool people is a mocker to God and His Words. You didn't know or see this because you are not in the Spirit of God. And they know that, this is why you can be fooled in believing that this is how you know that they are saved, by speaking in made-up and learned tongues and you fell for it because everyone is doing it. The reason that you fell for this lie is because you haven't read for yourself, or your eyes are blinded by the fact that you need a bandage to help the healing of your problems. You are blinded by the creature and not the creator. See, that was a gift of the Holy ghost that was giving to the disciples on that day because they was going to be talking to a lot of different nations of people that spoke different languages. In order for God's words to be carried out, they had to be able to communicate with the different people in their own languages. Wow, what an awesome God.

Even though Christ lives within you, your body will die because of sins, but your spirit and soul will live, for Christ has pardoned or forgave your sins. And if the Spirit of God, who raised up, Jesus from the dead lives in you. He will make your dying bodies live again after you die by means of this same Holy Spirit living within you. So, this means that you don't owe your sinful nature anything that it begs for. For if you keep on following your sins, you are lost and will perish for eternal hell. But if through the power of the Holy ghost it kills the deeds of the flesh and you shall enter into God's rest. You must admit that we are sinners living in sin, we must repent for all of our sins and ask forgiveness for what we have done wrong in our life. Turn from your sins and seek Jesus' face, read His words and learn of Jesus to get a personal relationship with Him. Obey His words and ask for the gift of the Holy ghost to keep you and teach you His ways. Do His will or purpose in life that He has for you. Gifts and the calling of God are without repentence (Romans 11:29). God will not change His mind about what He has called you to do. If God has called you, that calling is still there, whether or not you have obeyed. And if God gave you a gift, if He gifted you along a certain line, then that gift is still there. Apostle Paul told Timothy to stir up the gift that was within him. If you want to walk out God's plan for your life, it's time to stir up that gift that is given to you.

CHAPTER 16

Wouldn't Mind Dying if Dying Was All

Take comfort and peace in mind knowing that death is not the end, but we can gain eternal life if we give our lives to Christ, then we will know that heaven is our home. We were not meant for this world alone, there was one barrier that separates us from eternal life is the wages of sins. Christ's promise is for all of us who truly puts your faith and trust in Jesus.

Matthew 16:28 tells us that there be some standing here, which shall not taste of death, till they see the Son of man coming in His kingdom. Going back up to the 24 verse through the 27 of Matthew when Jesus was preparing His disciples. He said these words, "If any man will come after me, let him deny himself and take up his cross and follow me. For whosoever will save his life shall lose it and whosoever will lose his life for my sake shall find it. For what is a man profited, if he shall gain the whole world and lose his own soul? Or what shall a man give in exchange for his soul? For the Son of man shall come in the glory of His Father with His angels and then he shall reward every man according to his works." This is saying to us that we must first decide not to have anything that we like and put it before Jesus, having all the pleasures and luxuries of life and not seeking Jesus for guidance and life. Take up your cross of all the suffering, trials, and tribulations of this world and follow Jesus to do the things that He had done in love, patience, and faith. Because if you stop doing all the things that are not like Christ, you will return back to your sins and lose your life. But if you give Jesus your life and allow Him to clean it up and live for Him, then you shall be saved and live for Him. The benefits and advantage of this world will cause you to lose your souls. And what do you have to give for exchange for your souls. Jesus is coming back to judge us and He wants His souls to be Holy, pure, and clean for the kingdom.

Let me give you a description of being born from your mother's womb. First, you must know that the very first man and woman was created by God and there is a possibility that God is speaking as a Trinity of the Father, Son, and Holy ghost. He said let us go and make man in our image, after our likeness, and let them have dominion over the fish of the sea and over the birds in the sky, over the livestock and all the wild animals, and over all the creatures that move along the ground. (Genesis 1:26) When He said create humans in our image does not mean that humans resemble Him physically (John 4:24) because God is a Spirit. God endowed humans with a certain kind of awareness, one which the animals and birds and fish were not given. Humans would possess the capacity for reason, morality, language, personality, and the ability to use morality and spirituality are unique to human beings among God's creations on earth. Like God, we would possess the capacity to experience and understand love, truth, and beauty. We are made in God's image in another way, as a model or a representative, God is the maker and all of creation belongs to Him. Now in the creation, God gave man the responsibility to rule over the other creations. Then during the process of life, while living in the garden that was prepared for the created humans, they did something that God told them not to do and that was disobey His rules of the garden. He also told them that if they do that, they would surly die. Well, you heard and read the story how that the two people that God had set aside to be perfect and live a full, abundant life disobeyed His rules. They were cast out of the garden to go and replenished the earth and labor for their food. Now this brings us to the place of everyone else being born from their mother's womb. Since we were born and not created, we were born into sin and shaped into iniquity. In order for us to be born and live, God had to breathe the breath of life into our souls. That's why we have the Spirit of God, but it is sinful because of the way we enter into this world by being born and not created. So, now we have two spirits in us, one to do good and the other to do bad. These two spirits are always waring one against the other. God gave us a choice to decide which way that we are going to live or which spirit we are going to choose to serve. We cannot serve two masters, you will love one and hate the other or serve one and not the other. God wants us to have a made-up mind about whom we are going to serve. He said in His words that He is a jealous God. (Exodus 34:14) For thou shalt worship no other god. Genesis 6:6-7 says that it repented the Lord that He had made man on the earth, and it grieved Him at His Heart. He said that He will destroy man whom I created from the face of the earth, both man and beast and the creeping thing and the fowls of the air; for it repenteth Me that I have made them. But one man found grace in God's eyes He had seen righteous before Him in that generation of Noah.

This is very scary and upsetting to know that God was going to kill out everything that He had made because of our stubbornness, hard headed, stiff neck people who does not want to obey or have someone or something controlling them. God can up with a plan to redeem man back to Him to be able to receive eternal life. And that's when Jesus came down from His throne of grace and died for all of our sins, so we can have the rights to the tree of life. Should we continue in sin that grace may abide? No, no, no.

Dying was a horrible thing until Jesus came on the scene. The grave would hold your souls for eternity with suffering and turmoil. When Jesus died on the cross, He went down into the grave and took the stain out of death and preached to the saints. The grave doesn't have any victory over our souls anymore because of Jesus Christ. His human soul didn't go to Sheol, which is a place of the souls of the dead, both righteous and the unrighteous. The word Sheol is translated as Hades, and the description of Sheol in the Old and New Testaments bear some resemblance to the Hades of Greek mythology. It is under the earth (Numbers 16:30-33) and it is like a city with gates and bars (Isaiah 38:10, Job 17:16). It is a land of darkness, a place where shades, the shadowy souls of men dwell. It is the land of forgetfulness, where no work is done and no wisdom exists. Sheol is a place where no one praises God. But the eyes of the wicked shall fail and they shall not escape, and their hope shall be as the giving up of the ghost. Now we that died have to be judged when the judgement day comes. Jesus said in John 14:48, "He that rejecteth Me, and receiveth not My words, hath one that judgeth him; the word that I have spoken, the same shall judge him in the last day." Wouldn't mind dying if dying was all. We have a purpose and a plan to be here on this earth. It is not for our own good but for God's will. We must all stand before Christ to be judged. So, what Jesus has came to show and tell us is that we have to give Him our lives in order for us to have eternal life with the Father. To live forever in love, peace, and happiness in Christ Jesus.

We are no longer under God's curse doomed forever for our sins. Some of us goes along with the crowd full of sins because it looks good and feels good to our souls. The devil who is the prince of the air and evil works is at work right now in the hearts of those who are so easy to be mislead. And the reason that you are easily mislead is because you will not try Jesus or give Jesus a chance to show and prove to you that He is a rewarder of those who diligently seek and serve Him. We are not alive in the body unless we give our whole life to Jesus, so He can take away, change, rebirth, and lead and guide us into Holiness for the kingdom of God.

Salvation is not a reward for the good that we have done, so none of us can take any credit for it. It is God Himself who has made us what we are and has given us a new life through Christ Jesus. Remember once long ago we were called heathens, unclean by the Jews. We were not taught about living Holy or righteousness before God. Since the Jews rejected Jesus when He came, that gave us a chance, too, we can get the promise that God made to them also.

Jesus has done and still is doing His Father's will, above all Jesus wishes that we all be saved and filled with the Holy ghost to live eternality with Him. Jesus died once for all of us to end sin's power, and now He lives, but He wants to live down on the inside of us. Lip service and false worship will not allow you to live fully in this world without Jesus inside of you. You are no longer tied to the law where sin enslaves you, but you are free under God's favor and mercy. Having a desire to change is the key to becoming a child of Jesus. People will tell you that they know about Jesus or that they already have Jesus. But they are not living the way of the Lord. Love is the first thing that Jesus asks us to do toward each other's. I found out that you can't have a gap of love without Jesus in your lives for real. Loving without Christ will fail you.

The battle of life is not fleshly but spiritually. Satan is real, angels, demons, they all exist, but we don't have to live in fear of the supernatural. We have a powerful weapon against temptation and accusation. God has given us His Word, to let us know who He is and who we are to know what is true.

Be strong in the Lord and in His mighty power. Put on the whole armor of God, so that you can be able to stand against the devil and his tricks and cons of the devil and his angels daily. Now you know that flesh doesn't last forever, but our souls do, we just have to decide where do we want our souls to rest, dying out of flesh is not all. Wouldn't mind dying if dying was all.

God is faithful and just, He will strengthen you and protect you from the evil sins of this world. But you have to give Him your life and die daily out of sins with the help of our Lord and Savior. I pray that you receive the Lord into your lives and live. May God continue to bless you in well doing.

CHAPTER 17

Relationships

I have decided to talk a little on relationships, whether you are married or just dating to become a couple for marriage. I have been married now this day, May the 20th, 2019 for 22 years with my soul mate for 25 years. I can brag on Jesus' union because He said in His words that, "wherefore they are no more twain but one flesh. What therefore God hath joined together, let no man put asunder." (Matthew 19:6) the word asunder means to break apart or pulled into two pieces. When you are married, you and your significant other becomes one flesh in the Lord. Marriage is honorable in all and the bed undefiled, but whoremongers and adulterers God will judge. (Hebrews 13:4) The word undefiled means not mad corrupt or impure or unclean. Let's look at the words whoremongers and adulterers. Whoremongers is a person who has dealings with prostitutes, especially a sexually pro- miscuous man. One who mongers with whores, who involves himself with prostitutes. This is an old fashion word that is mainly found in the King James Version in the Bible. The next one, adulterers, is voluntary sexual intercourse between a married person and a person who is not his or her spouse. Now the reason that these two people are doomed of judgement because God has told and showed us how to live and react to our sexual natural. Fornication is a sin before God. We know that He is the one who made male and female genital parts, but we must also know that He is the one who tells us how to or when to use it the right way for Him. Fornication is sexual intercourse between people not married to each other. There are laws against all of these sexual pleasures that are keeping us from serving God like He said for us to do. Now this is the way you will have to have Jesus to keep or kill the deeds of the flesh that are keeping you from receiving Him fully. God will not come into an unclean body or vessel. God does not have anything to do with sins. I said all of that to say this, that it is better for you to marry than to commit any sins against Christ Jesus. But if you feel that you don't need any companion to be complete, then your best out is to get Jesus in your life and let Him kill the deeds of the flesh. Because a man cannot take fire on his chest and not get burned. See, we need the Lord in every walks of life. Every marriage situation is different and special to the individual person. I am blessed to have been given the man for me. It took Jesus and some understanding, trust, communication, and forgiving for us to have lasted this long with love between us. Women are strong willed human beings and they all wants to be loved. But some of us don't know how or what love is. One thing for certain and two things for sure is that God is love. You don't have to wait until Jesus saves both of you in order to serve Him. He said that the wife can save the husband and the husband can save the wife. See, it is still your choice to decide whom are you going to serve, Jesus or the devil.

Women were made to be help meet to the man, but in this day and time, we tend to want to take over the men work and not do what we were made to do. I understand that we have grown stronger and wiser in this age of life, but it is still God's way or no way at all. See, when we leave from the way that it was supposed to be, then we start to invent our own ways of life. Now you see that our ways don't work out for us. We want our equal rights to men and not to God. To be with different opinions doesn't mean that you are wrong or right, it just simply means that you have a mind to express your thoughts and feelings about the situations. I have learned that being married is the best thing that ever happened to me for my life. At first, when we were married for just one year, I was so independent that I thought I didn't need help from my spouse to make any decisions concerning us. But I got a rude awakening from him sitting me down and we communicated about what we are supposed to be doing with each other's help. Ladies, we don't have to have the last say so on everything, we have to trust in our spouses to make the right decisions concerning our well-being. Now I am not telling you to be silent on every issue, but some things does not requires your input. If you don't have Jesus first involved, trust, communication, and understanding, then it is very hard to get along or continue the relationship. My next book will have more details and information concerning healthy relationships. I just had to give you a little insight of what it means to serve God with your whole hearts. Because relationships play a very big part in life's journey. You will not serve Jesus with a pure heart doing the things the flesh wants. Pray, asked, trust in Jesus to send or mend a great relationship for you to become a beautiful married woman for God. When we stand and take our vows, we are vowing before God to love, honor, cherish, and obey in sickness and in health. Be wise as a serpent and humble as doves.

Follow peace with all men and holiness, without which no man shall see the Lord (Hebrews 12:14).

This is a story from Matthew 20: 1-16 and it reads, "For the kingdom of heaven is like unto a man that is a householder, which went out early in the morning to hire labourers into his vineyard." This is telling us that heaven has an owner who is God and He came down from His throne to find servants to work in this world, which is His vineyard which belongs to Him, not us. This world belongs to God, we are just pilgrims passing through in the flesh. And when he had agreed with the labourers for a penny a day, he sent them into his vineyard. Our reward or pay is life eternal with Him forever. That is the agreement that He made with us if we are His workers or servants. He also went out and about the third hour and saw others standing, idle in the marketplace, and said unto them, go ye also into the vineyard, and whatsoever is right, I will give you. And they went their way. Now Jesus has chose and hired you to work for Him, but He also made room for others to work in the world for Him, too. There are a lot of people just living here and not doing anything or serving anybody just laying around doing nothing. He said in His words whosoever will let him come. (Revelation 22: 16-17) This water of life is freely given. And he went out about the sixth and ninth hour and did likewise. About the 11th hour, he went out and found others standing idle and saith unto them, why stand ye here all the day idle? Jesus wants to know why we are not doing anything productive or constructive with the time on this earth that He has given us. But they replied that no man hath hired us. He the vineyard owner saith unto them, go ye alo in the vineyard; and whatsoever is right that shall ye receive. Meaning that whatever Jesus has promised us as a reward or pay that the ones who just came to Him, Jesus, to work will get the same pay eternal life. So, when even was come, the lord of the vineyard saith unto his steward, call the labourers and give them their hire, beginning from the last unto the first. And when they came that were hired about the 11th hour, they received every man a penny. But when the first came, they supposed that they should have received more and they likewise received every man a penny. But when they had received it, they murmured against the good man of the house. Well, our thoughts, and minds are not like Jesus. We feel and think that because we were first and had done the most work that our pay should be more than the ones who have just came aboard or been working for the Lord. But you will find out by continuing to read the scriptures that we don't own God's world or His people. He has made us equal to each other. Jesus asks us daily is it not lawful for Him to do what He will with that is His own? We belong to God and He can do whatever He wants to do, but whatever it is that He does, it is done right and true toward us. I told you that there is no respect of person in Christ Jesus. Then He asked is thine eye evil because He is good? There is no good but God. So, the last shall be first and the first shall be last: for many be called but few chosen. Don't you worry about your pay because everyone that has been hired will not stay or stand steadfast, unmovable, always abiding in God's word. He has called a whole lot of us, but many of us will not be able to stand or trust in Jesus. The one's that are chosen will stand still and see the salvation of the Lord for eternal pay. We must get a personal relationship with God. He is married to us and we got to come to the feast there's a wedding going on and the Bridge groom is ready to say, "I do" to the bride, which is you. He says until death do us part on this earth, then we will reign together in Heaven for everlasting life together. Jesus and us. Together forever. 2 Corinthians 6:14 tells us not to be unequally yoked together with unbelievers: for what fellowship hath righteousness with unrighteousness? And what communion hath light with darkness? This is dealing with Christians being joined together with unbelievers in an ungodly way. This should not be or try avoiding. This term yoked comes from ancient biblical tines where two oxen would be joined together with a yoke. The yoke was the wooden piece that went around their necks, so they could be teamed up and controlled. If one ox was weaker than the other, then they were considered unequally yoked and would not be able to perform well together. So, Apostle Paul's writing because he was dealing with the paganism found in the Corinthian area. The word paganism means a religious movement incorporating beliefs or practices from outside the main world religions, especially nature worship.

We are using the bible scriptures to help us to decides whether or not we should stay together or leave. But don't really know what the words are truly saying. Here is another scripture that is used to break up a relationship after you have been married. God didn't choose him or her for me, that's why he or she is not my spouse anymore. Well now, remember the verse what God joined together, let no man put asunder. We are doing this daily to get out of, so we can do what we want to do and not what Jesus wants us to do for as getting or being married.

Choose your partners wisely, here are some questions to ask yourself while you are deciding to married:

- Is he or she born again?

- Is he or she a one man woman, or one woman man?

- Does he or she honor their parents?

- Do they take care of their younger sister, brother, or children?

- Are they walking with God?

- Are they in church and subject to leadership?

- Do they read the bible or pray with me?

- Do they have a job?

- Are they in debt?

- Does he or she have wholesome friends?

- Does he or she have a good reputation?

If the answers to any of these questions is no, then these are some matters for concern. Investigate the reasons why you are getting a no to these questions. Because you must choose your future spouse wisely. In order to adhere to what God's words tell us to do as being married.

Again, I will say this: Wisdom is to fear God, knowledge is to know what the words are saying to you, and understanding is to cease from sins. Father, Son, Holy ghost. Trinty of the God Head – In all of your getting on this earth, get an understanding. The reason that we all are not saved yet is because we are perishing from lack of understanding of the Words of God.

> I PRAY THAT YOU WILL BE BLESSED
> AFTER READING THIS BOOK,
> AND I PRAY THAT YOU WILL SEARCH OUT
> WHAT YOUR PURPOSE IS ON THIS EARTH.
> WE ALL HAVE A PURPOSE AND PLAN
> FOR OUR LIVES WHILE THE BLOOD
> IS STILL RUNNING WARM IN OUR VEINS.

CHAPTER 18

Faith Without Works is Dead

What is faith? The bible tells us that faith is the substance of things hoped for and the evidence of things not seen. (Hebrews 11:1) Meaning that we hope for the Holy ghost to be saved or any other things of Christ that we need to gain eternal life with Him, Jesus. We must believe that Jesus can save us to live for Him. We don't know when or how that He is going to do it, but we trust in Jesus to bring it to pass. Not doubting that He can't remove sin out of our lives. Through us having faith, we understand that the worlds were framed by the word of God, so that things which are seen were not made of things which we do see or appear. For without faith, it is impossible to please God, for he that cometh to God must believe that He is God and also that He is a rewarder of them that seek Him, constantly always looking and searching for Him daily.

Enoch, Noah, Abraham, Sarah, these are just some names of the ones who had faith in whatever it was that God told them what He was going to do for them. We also be warned of things not seen, but do we trust in our own faith in Jesus? Even Moses had to have faith in God in order to help the people that were slaves in Egypt to be free from bondage. By faith Moses left the wrath of the king and kept his eyes on the invisible God whom he could not see. Through his faith, the Passover was kept, he did as the Lord had told him to do by sprinkling of blood over the doors of the houses who he wanted God to spare. They went through the Red sea on dry land, the walls of Jericho came down; by faith the harlot Rahab did not perish with the people in Egypt when she had received the spies with peace. There is nothing impossible with God, He can do all and anything that He wants to do. Daniel in the lion's den, how God shut the mouth of the lion so they wouldn't be eaten up alive.

Let every man be swift to hear, slow to speak, also slow to wrath or anger.

The question was asked of God, what doth it profit anyone, though you say that you have faith, and have not works? Can faith save him? No, it cannot. That just like you saying that you want a job but never goes out to find or seek one. Will you get hired? No, so faith works the same way with trying to get saved. You see then how that by works a man is justified and not by faith only. Even if you have faith alone, it is dead without works. We put works into all of the worldly stuff that we does; for example, we makes plans for holidays and birthdays by preparing for it or going about and buying things for that day. So, we know what faith is, it's just that we use our faith in the wrong areas of life for our own good. Because we do not know what shall be on the morrow. What is our lives, it is a vapor that appeareth for a little time and then vanisheth away. For we should say if it's the Lord's will, we shall live and do this, or that.

Confess your sins to Jesus and trust Him to take them away and kill the deeds of the flesh. To live Holy and righteousness before Jesus. We have an weapon in our mouths that cannot be tamed but by Jesus. It is the tongue can no man tame it. It is unruly evil and full of deadly poison that is being used in the wrong way. We need to ask Jesus to put a bit in our mouths and bridle down our tongues, so we can use it for His glory and purpose of service to God. Faith is the key to have this thing done unto you, the bit and bridle from God.

We are always asking amiss of things to consume upon our lust of our flesh. Submit yourselves therefore to God, and trust that He will save you. You ask and receive not because you don't trust or believe that He can or will do it. Faith also brings about patience for the things that you have asked Jesus to do in your lives. When you ask Jesus for anything for yourselves, you have to wait on Him to bring them to past.

I truly had faith that one day, I didn't know when or how, that I would be saved. But I had to seek after salvation from Jesus. How I did it was starting to pray, read, fast, and meditate on His words and Him, Jesus. But while I was waiting for the change in my life, I kept the faith that He was going to do it. Now I didn't get saved while I was having faith. I was in the world doing the things of the world, doing whatever my flesh called for that was not God. So, I prolonged the Saving process and went about doing my thing, which I thought was right for me. But I was wrong and didn't want to get saved at the time of my sinning. I had to study and learn that He, Jesus, wanted me to come to Him while I was still yet sinning. I thought that I had to put the saving of my soul on hold until I was ready to give Jesus my whole life. Then I found out that He wanted me to come while I was sinning, so He can remove, clean, and set my sinful soul free.

CHAPTER 19

Forgiveness

The word forgiveness as a conscious, deliberate decision to release feelings of resentment or vengeance toward a person or group who has harmed or wrong you, regardless of whether they actually deserve your forgiveness. Now people will tell you that it does not mean forgetting, nor does it mean condoning or excusing offenses. But Jesus tells us that He do not say up to seven times but up to 70 times seven. (Matthew 18:22) For if you forgive men, their trespasses, your heavenly Father will also forgive you. But if you do not forgive men, their trespasses, neither will your Father in heaven forgive your trespasses. (Matthew 6:14-15) Forgiving others is important, but sometimes it can be really difficult or hard to do. You might ask yourselves these questions. Why should I forgive, and how can I do it? The bible is crystal clear on the necessity of it. There are no caveats, such as unless, if, or but. Jesus Christ suffered unrighteousness, no one could have suffered more unrighteously than Jesus. Some of his last words on the cross were, "Father, forgive them, they know not what they do."

Forgiveness is the act of pardoning; the word pardon means to forgive. The Hebrew and Greek words translated, forgive falls into two general and overlapping meanings. The first refers to financial matters and involves the annulment of the obligation to repay what is owed. (Matthew 18:15)

If your brother or sister or anybody sins against thee, go to him privately and confront him about his faults. If he listens and confesses it, you have won back your brother. If not, then take someone with you to witness and ask him again. But if he still refuses, then take him or the situation to the church. And if he doesn't accept what the church has said, then excommunicate him from the church. If you forgive on earth, you will be forgiven in heaven. Because whatever you freed on earth will be freed in heaven. We don't want to forgive people for what they had done against us, but we want people to forgive us for what we has done to them. Example of this is a servant owed his king $3,000 dollars and couldn't pay the debt. The King ordered him to be sold for the debt owed, also to sell his wife and children and everything that he owned. But the man fell down in the dirt and asked the King to be patience with him, that he will repay it all. Then the King was filled with pity, concerning the man and released him and forgave his debt. The same man who owed the King went to a man that owed him $2,000 dollars and grabbed the man by the throat and demanded his money. The man did the same thing that he had done to the King and fell down in the dirt, begging him for a little more time to pay. He asked him to be patient and he will pay. But no, the man wouldn't, he had the man arrested until the debt would be paid in full. The man who owed his friend went to the king and told him what the man that he had forgave had done. So, the king called the man before him and said, "You evil hearted man, I forgave you of a debt much more than what is owed you just because you asked me to. Shouldn't you have mercy on others, just as I had mercy on you." Then the angry king sent the man to the torture chambers until he paid every last penny due. This is what God will do to us if we truly refuse to forgive our brothers and sisters.

The other forgiveness meaning is much more frequent and concerns the reestablishment of an interpersonal relationship that has been disrupted through some misdeed. In Genesis 50:17, Joseph is implored by his brothers to forgive the evil that they did to him. Both of the meaning is applied to God's gracious pardoning of people's transgressions. Notice how the two verses in the Lord's Prayed in Matthew 6:12, Luke 11:14 - God is asked to forgive debts. There is a metaphor that is used to express forgiveness of sins. Psalms 51 is where David wrote this after Nathan the prophet had inform Davis of God's judgement against him because of his adultery with Bathsheba, and his murder of Uriah her husband. Davis was asking God to blott out, to wash, purging, and to hide his face. There are more forgiveness asking in Isaiah 38:17, Jeremiah 31:34, and Micah 7:19. He will tread our iniquities under His foot, cast all our sins into the depths of the sea. These expressive phrasing highlights the completeness of God's forgiveness, which is served as model for our human conduct.

Luke 6: 31-16 tells us to treat others as you want them to treat you. Do you think that you deserve credit for merely loving them or those who love you? No, sinners do that, too, so why should you get credit? That don't set you apart from them. Is that wonderful, that what sinners do if you lend money only to those who can repay you, what good is that? None, verse 35 in the book of Luke says love your enemies, do good to them, lend to them. And don't be concerned about the ones that can't or won't repay you. Then and only then your reward will be great in heaven. This is one of the laws of God that we must obey in order to make it in. Pay attention to this teaching of Jesus. Judge not, this is saying to us to stop and don't never criticize or condemn anyone. It will all come back on you. If you give, you will get forgiveness. Yes, now you see it all, it is good for you to undergo or go through bitterness and suffering. Because Jesus has lovingly delivered us from death by forgiving all of our sins. Long time ago, you didn't have to or it wasn't necessary to admonish one another to know the Lord. Everyone, both small and great, shall really know God and His Son Jesus. Everyone was hell bound when Jesus came. He fulfilled the laws and forgave all of us for our sins. All things are possible to him who believes said Jesus Christ all things (Mark 9:23).

When you don't have the power, when you know that it is not in you to forgive, then you must find it in Jesus. Does this mean that the forgiving negate the pain you have suffered? Does it reverse the things that have happened to you, or does this mean the person who has wronged you doesn't have to take responsibility for his/her actions? No, but you will be free from the thoughts of hatred and bitterness and the burden they are. Forgiveness is for your sake, not only for the sake of the one who you are forgiving. When you do forgive, you don't have to live with the burden. You should forgive regardless of their attitude. Their sins are between them and God. We have to stand and be judged for ourselves, can't no one stand for us. God is righteous above all else. But judgment and vengeance belongs to God. Forgiveness is not a feeling, it is a choice. When you choose to forgive, you will have to go to God on your knees for the power to forgive. Then you are choosing not to let hatred rule in your hearts.

Take all of your burdens to the Lord because He cares for you. This is why we must receive the gift of the Holy ghost because the power of forgiveness is from the Holy Spirit. Forgive and forget goes hand in hand. Forget is to lose one's memory of disregard. If you don't forget, then the problems and burdens are still in your hearts and on your shoulders. Jeremiah 31:34 tells us that they shall teach no more every man his neighbor and every man his brother, saying know the Lord; for they shall all know me, from the least of them unto the greatest of them. For God will forgive their iniquity and Jesus will remember their sins no more. This act shows the righteousness of God and makes salvation real. The benefits of forgiving one another is spiritual cleansing, restored love, and freedom as a Christian. There were several examples of spiritual people whom had to forgive others. Jesus was the perfect example, Esau and Jacob, Joseph, Moses, David and Solomon, what about Paul and Stephen. This action made them better and greater for the rewards from Jesus our Savior.

So, yes, you see that it is very important in your walk with Jesus to forgive and forget the things or persons who has wronged you.

CHAPTER 20

Calling Upon God in Distress

The word distress is an affliction or suffering of something or someone. In times of your distress, just call upon the Lord Jesus and He will hear your cry. He will give you the comfort to your soul in knowing that Jesus is a rewarder of those who seek Him daily. In trouble and out of troubles.

BLESS, BLESSED, BLESSINGS—

Before we begin to discuss distress, look and see what the words say about being bless, blessed, and blessings.

Bless is to bestow happiness or prosperity upon praise and glorify.

Blessed is the past tense of bless, the objects of God's favor. The reason for being blessed is that you are chosen, or you believe, or are forgiven, justified or chastened to keep God's words. These few verses in the bible will explain the difference in the blessed. Ephesians 1:3-4 for chosen, Galatians 3:9 for believe, Psalms 32: 1-2 for justified, Romans 4:6-9 for chastened, and Revelations 1:3 for keeping God's words.

Blessing is the gift and approval of God; it's a blessing to wake up this morning. It's a blessing to be in the house of the Lord. It's a blessing to be closed in your right mind. It's a blessing to have food to eat. It's a blessing to have clothes to wear. It's a blessing to have the activities of your limbs. It's a blessing to have a roof over your heads. It's a blessing to be chosen by God.

There are spiritual and eternal blessings:

Salvation - John 3:16

Election - Ephesians 1:3-5

Regeneration - 2 Corinthians 5:17

Forgiveness - Colossians 1:14

Adoption - Romans 8: 15-17

No condemnation - Romans 8:1

Holy Spirit, Ghost - Acts 1:8

Justification - Acts 13:38-39

New covenant - Hebrews 8: 6-13

Fatherly chastisement - Hebrewa 12:5-11

Christ intercession - Romans 8: 3-14

Perseverance - John 10:27-29

Glorification - Romans 8:30

You got to know and believe that God is real, He is a spiritual being and self-made. He is a holy God, He said holy without no man shall see the Lord. Now knowing this, we must call upon Him when we are in distress or troubled. He said let not your hearts be trouble, this was Jesus talking to all of us. For us to know that He has been given the same power as His Father God. Look at the book of Psalms, the 18th chapter starting at verse 1-5. David is saying, "Oh, how I love Jesus, why? Because He has done such tremendous things for me." Now we can relate to David's cry for the wonderful things that God has done in his life and ours. He also goes alone and says the Lord is my fort and my stronghold, where I can enter and be safe; no one can follow me in and slay me. My rescuer, He saves us from evil. He delivers us from trials, evil, and from death. He, Jesus, is my Savior, my power a rock where none not even the devil can reach me. A tower of safety. I can put my confidence in Jesus, He is my shield, He is like the strong horn of a mighty fighting bull. All you need to do is cry to Him, Jesus. Oh, praise the Lord and you will be saved from all of your enemies.

Before Jesus came and died for us, death bound us with chains, the souls could not have a resting place. We were afraid to die because of the bound. The floods of falseness and lies, discard for God's truth mounted a massive attack against us. The grief of sadness of eternal torment encircle and travel around us. David felt trapped of death and helpless. The feeling of dying had him ready to die. When you call upon the Lord, who is worthy to be praised. He will save you from all of your enemies. The waves of death are a feeling that moves back and forth. It is a swelling feeling that you cannot release, it surrounds you. I don't where you go or do, the feeling is there. Evil bursts upon you, causing you to feel like killing yourself or dying out, giving up on life. Call upon Jesus, He is our help. He will hear you from His temple. Make sure that your cry reaches His ears by giving Him your lives.

When you call on Jesus in distress, with an earnest heart, sorrow in your souls. Stuff happens, spiritual stuffs happens. The earth rocks and reeled, the mountains shake and tremble. Jesus is coming to help you. The devil trembles and flee or run from the helping coming from Jesus. Satan knows who is coming when Jesus gets angry or wroth with strong anger. There is a reward of righteous for the ones who obey Him. Sometimes your enemies be so strong that you be helpless in their hands. That's when the devil comes to you on your weakest days. But if you stay steady in Jesus, He will lead you to a safety place in Him.

The Lord rewards you for doing right, must follow His commands. Stop sinning and turning your backs on Jesus because you are going to need the Lord in your life to be able to withstand the wiles of the devil. God knows who are real or not because He watches every step that we takes in life. Now with God's strength, you can scale any wall, attack any troops of demons or devil.

So, when you are in distress, call upon Jesus. He will deliver us from all of our enemies. When you suffer, you are not suffering alone. Jesus sufficed His self for all of the distress and suffering that we will have during this journey of life. The devil does things to us for bad, but God turns it into our good. There is a story about how the devil tries to turn your good into bad. That is the story of Esther and her cousin Mordecai. When they went on a journey for a better life, Esther didn't reveal to the King that she was a Jew, fearing the pain and suffering that will be put upon them if they had told who they were. But she had to tell the truth to the King in order for God to bless them with a blessing. In the book of Numbers 32:23 tells us about how the people wanted to keep what God was giving them, but they had to be guiltless before the Lord. We must stay in the way of the Lord and do right and try to live right because be sure your sins will find you out. Whatever you do, do well and honestly with truth. We don't have the time that we think that we do. No matter what you are doing or into, find Jesus, so you will have help in your distress and suffering of the trials and tribulations of this He will give us later. For we all are waiting, praying, and hoping that when God resurrect His children for judgment, we will receive eternal life with Him, Jesus. The things that over came the world against its will at God's command will all disappear, and the world around us will share in the glorious freedom from sin which God's children will enjoy.

For on that day, thorns and thistles, sin, death, and decay will be done away with. Animals, plants, and things of the nature suffer in sickness and death as the await this great event. Even us as Christians, although we have the Holy Spirit within us as a foretaste of what we can continue to have in the future glory. We also groan to be released from pain and suffering. We, too, wait anxiously for that day when God will give us our full rights as His children. Including the new bodies He has promised us. Bodies that will never be sick or never die. We are saved by trusting in Jesus, this means looking forward to getting something we don't have yet. Because a man that already have something doesn't need to hope and trust that he will get it. If we keep on trusting God for something that we don't have yet, it will teach us how to wait patiently and confidently on Jesus. And in the same way by our faith, the Holy Spirit of God helps us with our daily problems and in our praying. For we don't even know what we should pray for. But Jesus prays for us with such feeling that it cannot be expressed in words. God knows all hearts, He knows what the Spirit is saying as He pleads for us with a harmony with God's own will. Everything is or has happened to us is working for our good. If we love God and are fitting into His plans.

From the beginning, God decided that those who came to Him and all along He knew who would. Should become like His Son, so that His Son would be the first with many brothers. Have chosen us, He called us to come to Him. And when we came, He declared us not guilty, filled with Christ's goodness. Gave us right standing with Himself and promised us His Glory. What can we ever say to such wonderful things as these? If God is on our side, who can be against us? Who then will condemn us? Will Christ? No, He is the one who died for us and came back to life again for us. He is sitting at the place of the highest honor next to God, pleading for us in heaven.

We must be ready to face death at every moment of the day, we are like sheep going to be killed. Despite all of this victory is ours through Jesus Christ, who loved us enough to die for us. Nothing can ever separate us from His love, death can't, and life can't, or the way that you live can't. The angels won't and all the power of hell itself cannot keep God's love or change His love for us. Nor your fears for today or your worries for tomorrow will. It doesn't matter how high or how deep you are in the world of troubles. Nothing will ever be able to separate us from the love of God. He demonstrated it by our Lord Jesus Christ when He died for us. We must Jesus bare this cross alone and all the world goes free?

So, don't be afraid of those who threaten you or how much you are suffering in this world. The time is coming when the truth will be revealed, everything that is done plotting in the darkness will become public information. Fear only God who can destroy both the body and our souls. Just to touch a little on our families, we might sometimes ask ourselves, why do they come against us. He, Jesus, told us that our first foes will be our families. The ones who are right in the household with you. We can't love mother, father, sister, or brother more than we love Jesus. We can't put no one or nothing before Jesus. The next time that you are in distress or feel like giving up. Try Jesus, tell Him all about it and He will work it out for your good. Praise Him for what He has already done, and praise Him for what He is going to do for you to be alright and heal. Stressing is not for you to own or achieve in your lives, give all of your worries and cares to the master up above. He cares and will not put more on you than you can bare.

My mother used to sing this song, What would my life be, if it wasn't for Jesus who blesses me in so many ways. I can say I thank you Jesus for being so good to me.

MAY YOU CONTINUE TO BE BLESSED IN WELL DOING. AMEN

THE CRYING BLACK CHILD:

While living inside my mother's womb
Feeling the sense of doom.

The anticipation of being born,
Wondering when life will come.

The water splashes through and through,
Sensing the tears isn't true.

Beginning to toss up and down,
Why do I have this frown?

I thought I felt a tear,
Oh, but it was very near.

The day has come for me to see,
That this experience is once be.

Head first,
Then the feet.

Why am I crying so discreet.
The child is here for everyone to see,

Thank God the child is me!

IT WAS GOD'S WILL

Dirt and clay, mud He formed man.
Breathe into the structure body because He can.

I am on a mission 311
Cannot tell you where it came from.

Help your fellow man with cheer,
Love him and hold him near.

I cannot do it without the I Am,
In myself it would be a sham.

You need me to need you,
In spite of everything we do.

I am wondering through the land,
Helping everyone I can.

It was God's will, for this to be.
I am on a mission can't you see.

To acquire this schedule from the start,
Tears and cheers, frowns and smiles.

While this mission will take awhile.
The years has grown old and so have I,

The will of this mission has the stakes so high.
It was God's will for this mission to be.

311 is what they call me.

NOBODY CAN FIX IT

I cried in the midnight hour, I cried in the morning light,
Hoping and praying that everything will be alright.

Trying to wait on the fix it man to come,
He was too busy to fit me in, but nobody can handle it,
Nobody can.

The morning has viewed the whole day,
I hoped that it would be this way.

The problems still linger over my head,
Waiting for the Fix it, you promised you said.

Toward my way it is hopeless to response.
To be ready and fixed was my goal.
Nobody showed of that's the lie you told.

Nobody showed up and all is well,
Midnight hours was just a spell.

THE LAST WILL

Give momma a kiss, and dad a big hug.
Remember the good times when we dance a jug.

Watch over each others as if I am still here,
Kept in step my spirit will be near.

You are and will always be in my heart,
Not till death do us apart.

Don't remove my items, or sell my worth,
Hang on to me for the stuff I left on this earth.

To pass it out to family will be my last will,
Even if it cost me just 1 dollar bill.

The items that I will leave don't cost a dime,
These gifts are precious than mine.

I give you Jesus in all of His glory,
So you can live to tell the story.

Of how He die for you and me,
This is what I want my last will to be.

To view it you have to be ready,
To accept the decision that I have chosen.

For my last will on this earth.
Try Jesus and see for yourself my child,

That you will need Him after awhile.

This last will is all I got,
To give you for the rest of your life.

MY MIND IS ROAMING

Writing down everything that comes to mind,
Thope this pen can keep up and don't be left behind.

I sit and think of all sorts of things to say,
Looked at the time it's still the same day.

Trying to do something constructive with myself,
Haven't found out who is this soul or is it an elf.

Been here before a long time ago,
My mind is roaming telling me what I am to know.

Making sense out of this mystery that is playing a part of my life,
I know I had hard times, and strife.

When I love, I love hard and long,
Want let go of the thought what could have gone wrong.

I need to be doing something that makes me content,
Cause life is not waiting on anyone consent.

Keep on roaming and I will hit the jackpot,
Of my mind's life spot.

KNOCK, KNOCK, WHO'S THERE

Someone is knocking at my door,
I got to answer with a smile, peeking in my heart's floor.

Okay, you can come in and have a seat,
Changing my attitude and the way I should be.

Don't stay to long because I haven't made up my mind,
If this is what I want on my line.

Who changed the program,
Or dimed the lights.
You are my company to enjoy these nights.

I decided to do it my way, and take over,
The structure of how this meeting seem like a three-leaf clover.

Going to sleep and sleeping through the night,
Knock, Knock who's there.
It's Jesus just seeing are you alright.

POETRY

My mind drifts out to the sea,
Trying to say some words or speak as soft as could be.

The brain plays a very important part,
All of the words come from the heart.

I see what you are thinking, it should say,
But the meaning is going another way.

Writer's block came calling yesterday,
I was so busy, I sent him away.

I can spite out and play the role,
Cause this is always from my soul.

Within my treasure chest is gold, platinum and silver,
These treasure never been bought with pain.

Poetry is what I am and always will be,
So, I give it sometimes to be free.

LOVE UNDER THE BIG TOP

I met my first love under the big top,
He was playing double diamond winning and couldn't stop.

I walked over and said hi,
and about that time a waitress came by.

He ordered me a drink, and got him a beer.
I'm so hot I'm staying right here.

He asked me my name, I told him Annie Jay,
He replied don't leave, I want you to stay.

The clowns was performing their little stunts,
I saw one clown he was as short as a runt.

I said to myself I'm glad I came because playing at
Circus turned out to be a lover's game.

He smiled at me with such a big grin and
gave me a token he said drop it in.

I pulled the handle as hard as I could,
the diamonds kept spinning like I knew they would.

I hit double sevens and won $200,
he grabs a cup and started gathering them up.

I'm glad I met my love at the big top, now we are coming back.
We can't stop! Gambling is a problem.

THE FLYING ELEPHANT

While dreaming in black and white,
I dream about an elephant that night.

Gray and whilt was his colors,
I was surprise of his statues.

He ran and flew so high,
Wondering how could this be.

I tossed and turned while I was sleep.
But this elephant flew passed me.

Then I was awakened with a loud noise,
The color of the dream kept me in the dark.

It was a flying elephant that was gray and white,
Why did I dream of this elephant tonight?

The noise I heard was an ambulance door,
When I open my eyes, I heard 1, 2, 3, 4
CLEAR.

CARNIVAL

Hear the laughter of the animals,
See the clowns dance and sing.

It must be the carnival near and close,
The ferry wheel turned round and round,
Up high and then to the ground.

I ran to the corner to see,
I want some fun in me.

Head hung down tears begin to fall,
It's in my mind that's all.

The lion roar with a great sound,
My stomach was turning upside down.

My eyes sparkler, the grind begins,
Happy me, happy me the Carnival is within.

HUSH LISTENING TOM

Shhhh!
Hush, I am trying to hear what I saw last year.

The voice is so low, I can't see,
I open my eyes and there was we,

Tom, I called him by his name,
I heard you should have came.
To my rescue, and my defense.

Wait a minute I see what I hear.
Shriving and shaken he came very near.

Shhhhh,
What, who can it be listening to my last year?

His name is Tom and he is my brain,
He said to my eyes come on out of the rain.

Whispering a thought and seeing the way,
Oh, I get it, it's just a new day.

THE RUIN FLOWER

Life takes you by surprise,
But you try to get some of its benefits.

Connecting to an I-V to survive.
Making sure your flower isn't deprived.

Every day the medicine flow through your stem,
Flow.

Spring up bright and early at sun rise,
Putting sun all over your leaves with care.
Checking your soil if you dare.

The night has fallen and it's over today,
The flower is ruin you should have gone your way.

Being still not uttering a word,
It's time to fold down the I-V.

Tomorrow is another chance to be.

FUNNI FACE

Twenty-five cents is what it cost,
To enter in don't get lost.

The old man with the cane in his hands,
Tap the table and said please stand.

A great big smile came across his face,
He looks with a polished funny face.

If you knew the processor, click and describe.
What you want to do while I shine my smile.

Theard step right up and let it ride,
But I couldn't move I wanted to hide.

Hurry, hurry, the show has begun,
Twenty-five cents is what it cost to come in.

A PRAIRIE'S WIFE

She has a bonnet on her head,
With bright dots.

She has a look of worry a woman,
She's not.

She has an apron over her dress,
With buttons in the front that looked a mess.

Red lipstick on her lips shining bright,
Hoping and wishing this is the night.

Turn around and look at me,
Tam not the one you think I should be.

Wine and dine me with your love,
Cause I was sent from heaven above.

Stand up and be what you were born to be,
That's what I thought until I found out differently.

A woman I am not, not even a wife,
But this prairie look got me cut with a knife.

Straight and deep down to the bone,
I think I better leave this alone.

I WONDER WHY?

You asked me a question,
I wonder why?

You told me a story,
I wonder why?

You showed me your secrets,
I wonder why?

Maybe it's a mystery to be solve,
I just keep getting deeper involve.

Maybe it's the way you are,
I really can't tell this far.

I wonder why is it deep from within,
I wonder, I wonder why?

It doesn't matter as long as you keep on
standing by.

BEAR BASKET

Smell a sweet and crisp day approaching,
The elements of love is in the air.

Fuzzy and cute is what I saw,
Hug me and squeeze me until satisfied.
The two handles on the basket is what I described.

Black and white is the colors of the day,
Red, yellow, and green is always in the way.

Apples, bananas, and pear,
Hoping that your love will still be there.

A sweet taste, a soft taste, and a sandy taste, too,
The bear basket is full threw and threw.

Take me by surprise and run through the fields,
Up and over the hills.

Let us adore the day as it travels on,
When night fall the basket is gone.

THE WONDERFUL WORLD OF PLAYERS

The game has begun, are you playing?
The tools has been set, can you obey them?

The contestants have been chosen,
Did you get pick?

Play fair and no cheating.
Let's start over because you weren't ready.

It is to be told, not sold.

You can get a refund as long as you play,
Let's began again but not this way.

Your turn has come to make your move,

Did you forget all the rule?

I'll go first, I'm not scared,
This is a wonderful world of players to be heard.

Slow down don't make your move to soon,
Cause if you do you will be shot to the moon.

The move was call, and you must not fall.
It is a wonderful world of players that's all.

IT WAS A LONG TIME AGO

My head was bowed down in sorrow,
You know the devil had me wrapped up in sin.

I started out to seek salvation,
I had a hard time resisting temptation.
I kept on searching till I found the king of king.

He changed my mind so I could think right,
Changed my heart, so I could love right,
Changed my feet, so I could walk right.

Yes, I found the king of king.
I found me somebody pick me up when I'm fallen down,
Built a fence all around me.

I kept on searching,
I was looking for peace of mind.
I was looking for joy divine.

Couldn't find peace nowhere,
Couldn't find love nowhere.

Yeah, yeah, I found the King of Kings.
It was a long time ago.

WHAT WOULD YOU DO IF GOD SAID I'M THROUGH?

What would you do, if God said that He was through,
Blessing, saving, and forgiving you.

Cried in the day time, even in the midnight hour,
I know that He can hear me with all of His power.

He asked me to pray, I said that I don't have time,
He asked me to love, you are a child of mine.

I told him this day can wait,
He said to me I don't hesitate.

To bless you with all your heart desire,
Come on and pray to me before you expire.

Are you through with me I quickly asked?
He said why wear that face like you are wearing a mask.

You can run, and run hard,
But I'm not through with you until you do your part.

I tried every day to do right,
but God you seem to hide from my sight.

I'm sorry, I'm so ashamed
I thought you heard my cry and call out my name.

I was wrong to treat you that way,
Today, I am ready not to play.

JESUS CHRIST IS HIS NAME

Jesus Christ is His name, some calls His Lord,
But they are the same.

He's seeking top position in your heart,
Just let Him come in from the start.

He founded the earth and established the heavens,
A place for your souls to live forever.

He formed man from the dust of the ground,
He is not lost, He's where He can be found.

He breathed into man the breath of life,
You don't have to go through this world with all of its strife.

He redeemed man from the curse of the law,
It was Him hanging on that tree, that's who I saw.

He only had one employer who is His Father,
Just call on Him, it's not a bother.

He never been tardy, absent, or late.
Try Him, Jesus, and add some more on your plate.

Healing the sick, brokenhearted, and setting the captive free,
Give your life to Jesus, then you will have liberty.

Wonderful counselor, authority, and power to cleanse your sins,
All you have to do is just let Him come in.

He laid down His life, so that we may live,
Defeated the archenemy, so you can heal.

Jesus Christ is His name,
Just call upon Him and don't be ashamed.

Believers and follower worldwide will testify,
That this man name Jesus is my kind of guy.

I MUST

I must love, I must be real.
Cause loving is a big deal.

I must care and treat you right,
when it gets dark, no one can fight.

I must show you how really I feel,
Loving you truly is a big deal.

I must laugh and cry with sincere,
I know that the end is near.

I must give Jesus my life and stay true,
I must live for Him until I am through.

I must forgive and forget,
If Jesus comes, I'm not ready yet.

I must do all that I can do,
To be the best for you.

I must, I must, I must is all I know,
When He calls my name, I must be ready to go.

I SAW TWO ANGELS

I saw two angels flying high above the clouds,
I rubbed my eyes to see that they were there.
Man, those angels were flying everywhere.

Chills ran down my spine, and I shook with fear,
Oh, Lord is the end near.

They were flying up and down around the clouds,
I saw two angels and then I started to frown.

Why I can't fly or have those wings,
I know that there is a spiritual place in between.

The wings was so white and big as can see,
Lord, I saw two angels how can this be.

For me to see the angels was a wonderful sight,
I pray that I will see them again tonight.